REVOLUTION VIA EDUCATION

AND OTHER ESSAYS

SAMUEL BLUMENFELD

CHALCEDON | VALLECITO, CA

*Revolution Via Education
and Other Essays*

Samuel L. Blumenfeld

Chalcedon
Vallecito, California
2009

Address all inquiries to:

Chalcedon
P. O. Box 158
Vallecito, CA 95251
U.S.A.

Library of Congress Cataloging-in-Publication Data

Blumenfeld, Samuel L.
Revolution Via Education and Other Essays
Samuel L. Blumenfeld
Includes index
ISBN-10: 1-891375-25-3
ISBN-13: 978-1-891375-25-5

Printed in the United States of America

First Edition

The essays in this collection were originally published in
*The Blumenfeld Education Letter, Chalcedon Report, The New American,
Imprimis,* and *WorldNetDaily*

For
Dorothy Rushdoony
*A Prophet's Companion
in Faith and Love*

Other Books
by Samuel L. Blumenfeld

*How to Start Your Own Private School,
and Why You Need One*

The New Illiterates

The Retreat from Motherhood

How to Tutor

*Alpha-Phonics: A Primer
for Beginning Readers*

Is Public Education Necessary?

NEA: Trojan Horse in American Education

The Whole Language/OBE Fraud

*Homeschooling: A Parents' Guide
to Teaching Children*

*The Victims of Dick and Jane
and Other Essays*

CONTENTS

PREFACE

I am delighted that Chalcedon has seen fit to publish a second collection of my essays, which were written over a number of years. As usual, education is the main subject of these writings, and as I mentioned in *The Victims of Dick and Jane*, the reader will find several themes and citations repeated in one form or another. In trying to reach as many readers in different audiences as possible, I found it imperative to bring to their attention some of the rather astounding writings I came across in my research.

In these essays I have tried to show how our country has been in the throes of an ongoing socialist revolution since the turn of the last century. And it has been engineered by real people with real names who consider themselves to be Americans but who have been doing all in their power to change the form of government given us by our Founding Fathers. The two major underpinnings of a socialist, ungodly, controlled society are public education and the income tax. We shall not be a free people until we get rid of both institutions.

Indeed, the prospects of maintaining our constitutional republic would be bleak if it weren't for the homeschool movement which, in my mind, is the most refreshing assertion of freedom-loving in America that has taken place in my lifetime. When I graduated from the City College of New York in 1950, I had been brainwashed to believe that socialism was inevitable. As a pro-capitalist, I didn't like that.

Why have so many educators and intellectuals chosen to prefer a "utopian" system of government that can only be imposed by coercion and the loss of freedom? The root of the problem is spiritual. When you reject God in favor of man's sovereignty, you not only lose the meaning of life, but you lose the principles that make a prosperous and free social order possible. And that is why a fierce battle is being waged between Christian homeschoolers, who place their faith in God's Word, and the public educators whose foolish and destructive notions are driving millions of American children insane.

I have been writing and lecturing about this for years, trying to wake up parents, and to my surprise, I've been somewhat successful. I am surprised by the number of parents who approach me at homeschool conventions and tell me that it was a lecture I gave some years back that convinced them to homeschool and that they want to thank me for it. One parent quoted something I had said seven years ago that impelled her to homeschool and which I had completely forgotten. But that thought had remained indelibly in her mind all those years. So I have ceased to underestimate my influence.

I am also most delighted by the parents who tell me how they taught their children to read using *Alpha-Phonics* and what great readers their children have become. I wrote that book especially for parents because I knew they needed a simple, easy-to-use reading program in order to do at home what the public schools had no intention of doing.

So there are rewards for laboring in the vineyard of educational freedom. Back in 1993, I spoke at Pensacola Christian College on the subject of multiculturalism. At the end of the lecture, a young lady, majoring in education, came up to me and broke down into tears as she spoke about her desire to help save children. And one young man, who waited patiently until everyone else had asked their questions, came up and shook my hand. He said he was a subscriber to my newsletter and appreciated my work. How can a writer not be affected by such reactions? And how could I not be impressed with the character and determination of these young Christians, eager to make a difference in their country?

My lectures have taken me to all fifty states, plus Australia, New Zealand, Canada, and Britain. Over the years I've been on hundreds of radio talk shows, but not on Oprah or any of the other national shows. I'm too politically incorrect.

But no one was more politically incorrect than Rev. R. J. Rushdoony. In my conversations with him, he stressed the importance of educating Christian children with a Bible-based curriculum. What particularly annoyed him was the fact that more than 80 percent of Christian parents patronized the ungodly government schools and were thus committing sin. He never minced words. Public education was bondage to the state. It was an acknowledgment that the state owned the children. To reinforce state control by patronizing and supporting the system was a sinful act, because God had commanded parents to educate their children in the love and admonition of the Lord.

That is why I am extremely grateful to Chalcedon, to Mark and Darlene Rushdoony, Susan Burns, and Andrea Schwartz for their appreciation of my efforts and for making the publication of this book possible. Hopefully, it will reach thousands of readers in the years ahead and leave indelible thoughts in their heads.

REVOLUTION VIA EDUCATION

I t is impossible to speak of the revolution that has taken place in American education since the 1930s without invoking the name of John Dewey. While it is true that many other important and influential personalities helped plan and carry out that revolution, their names are virtually unknown to the public. Who remembers James McKeen Cattell or Edward L. Thorndike or Charles H. Judd?

But everyone remembers John Dewey, whose memory has been kept alive by an army of devoted disciples. Why? Because John Dewey is the Lenin of the American socialist revolution, honored and revered by his followers very much in the way that Lenin was worshipped by the Communist party of the Soviet Union. Stalin may have been periodically denounced by Soviet leaders, but Lenin, who was every bit as evil, was and is still held up as the paragon of revolutionary virtue.

There are interesting similarities between John Dewey and Lenin. Both men have been deified by their disciples. Neither man is ever blamed for the failures of the system he helped bring into existence. And just as Lenin did not invent communism, John Dewey did not invent socialism. In fact, Dewey seldom used the word. He preferred the word "democracy" which he defined in his own special way. And that is why it is so easy for Dewey's disciples to refer constantly to their revolutionary mentor in the name of democracy. After all, who can possibly be against democracy, particularly if your concept of it is somewhat vague and ambiguous?

It was Robert Welch, founder of the John Birch Society, who decided that Americans ought to become unconfused about democracy. He coined the slogan: "This is a republic, not a democracy. Let's keep it that way." This simple formulation has helped thousands of Americans to reeducate themselves. And anyone who does this becomes acutely aware of how the enemy has used the distortions and confusion of language to gain his totalitarian ends. It was George Orwell who predicted how language would become so perverted by the collectivists that in time despotism would be called democracy, slavery freedom, and war peace.

Another great similarity between Dewey and Lenin is that both men were master strategists who studied closely the social systems they wanted to overthrow and came up with far-reaching plans whereby their respective revolutions could be carried out. Of course, Russia and the United States differed greatly as societies, and therefore the revolutionaries faced different realities. However, both Dewey and Lenin shared basic philosophical premises. They both rejected belief in God, both became materialists, both believed in evolution—that human beings were animals—and both believed in behavioral psychology as the means of studying human nature and controlling human behavior. Both men belonged to the world socialist movement, which by the late nineteenth century had diverged into two separate movements based on differing strategies.

The social democrats chose to use the legislative, parliamentary means to achieve socialism; and the communists advocated violent overthrow of the existing capitalist system and the establishment of a dictatorship of the proletariat. Even though the French Revolution was held up by socialists as their model of revolution, it was the catastrophe of the Paris Commune of 1871, in which 20,000 people were killed by government troops in a week of street fighting, that convinced socialists in Western Europe to resort to the parliamentary method to achieve their ends.

Probably the same would have been true in Eastern Europe had not World War I produced the conditions in which violent revolution could succeed. In the case of Russia, however, it should be remembered that the czar was deposed by a bloodless revolution led by the social democrat Alexander Kerensky. It was Lenin who then overthrew the weak provisional, but essentially democratic, government of Kerensky in October 1917 and established the communist regime with its reign of terror.

In Great Britain the socialist movement made little headway until the formation of the Fabian Society in 1884 by a small group of young intellectuals and professionals. With their religious beliefs virtually demolished by Darwinism and science, these young idealists needed some greater cause to live for, and many of them found it in socialism. The uniqueness of the Fabian Society was in its *modus operandi*. As Rose Martin wrote:

> The Fabian Society's originality lies in the techniques it has developed for permeating established institutions and penetrating political parties in order to win command of the machinery of power. Historically speaking, perhaps its most remarkable feat has been to endow social revolution with an aura of lofty respectability.

The Society had been named after the Roman general and dictator, Quintus Fabius Maximus, who became known as the Delayer because of his delaying tactics used against Hannibal in the second Punic War during the third century B.C. By avoiding all-out battles at a time when Rome was weak, Fabius won time to build up Rome's military strength. When Rome was finally ready, Hannibal was decisively vanquished and Carthage destroyed.

The Fabians stressed the value of delayed action. Fabian Tract No. 1 put it in these words: "For the right moment you must wait, as Fabius did most patiently when warring against Hannibal, though many censured his delays; but when the time comes, you must strike hard, as Fabius did, or your waiting will be in vain and fruitless."

On the cover of many Fabian publications was the motto: "I wait long, but when I strike, I strike hard." The tortoise became the heraldic device of the Society because it symbolized persistence, longevity, slow and guarded progress towards a revolutionary goal.

The three legendary leaders of the Fabian Society were Sidney and Beatrice Webb and George Bernard Shaw. Other important members were Theosophist Annie Besant, sexologist Havelock Ellis, Graham Wallas, who later taught at Harvard where he recruited Walter Lippmann to the cause, and H. G. Wells who eventually defected, calling the Fabians the New Machiavellians. Shaw is said to have confided to a German socialist friend that he had wanted the Fabians to be "the Jesuits of socialism."

In 1910, when the Society was twenty-five years old, Shaw commissioned an artist to design and construct a stained-glass window for the Society's headquarters. For thirty years the window was privately displayed to the socialist inner circle, for in the middle of it was the Fabian coat-of-arms: a wolf in sheep's clothing. It also depicted Sidney Webb and George Bernard Shaw as blacksmiths about to smash the world with sledgehammers, beneath the inscription, "Remould it nearer to the heart's desire," taken from a quatrain in Edward Fitzgerald's translation of Omar Khayyam:

> Dear Love, couldst thou and I with fate conspire
> To grasp this sorry scheme of things entire,
> Would we not shatter it to bits, and then
> Remould it nearer to the heart's desire.

Today the window can be seen by visitors to the Beatrice Webb House in Surrey, England, a memorial financed by the world socialist movement.

In 1887, the Fabian Society published its credo, to which every member was obliged to subscribe. It read:

> The Fabian Society consists of Socialists. ...It aims at the reorganization of society by the emancipation of land and Industrial Capital from individual and class ownership, and the vesting of them in the community for the general benefit.... The Society accordingly works for the extinction of private property in land.... The Society further works for the transfer to the Community of such Industrial Capital as can conveniently be handled socially. For the attainment of these ends the Fabian Society looks to the spread of Socialist opinions, and the social and political changes consequent thereon....

The main strategy of the Society was to develop, through permeation of the educated class, a socialist elite. Fabians insisted from the start that in advanced capitalist countries like England and the United States, socialism must begin at the top and meet the working masses halfway. Hence, great emphasis was put on the development of leadership, particularly among academics. In 1894, the Fabians established the London School of Economics and Political Science, which was to become the training ground for the socialist elite.

The Fabian idea was not unique to Great Britain. In the United States a similar strategy was outlined in a book entitled *The Cooperative Commonwealth*, written by a socialist lawyer named Laurence Gronlund and published in 1884, the very year the Fabian Society was founded. Gronlund, a Danish immigrant who was educated in Europe, had come to the conclusion that neither European methods nor an alien terminology could ever succeed in making socialism acceptable to most Americans. Social revolution had to be disguised, he said. It had to be a gradualist movement for social reform. To the average American of the 1880s, the word "socialism" was synonomous with atheism, revolution, and free love.

But among the academic elite, where sympathy for socialism was far greater than among the common folk, it was a different story. Among those sympathetic to socialism was Professor Richard T. Ely of Johns Hopkins University. It was Ely who organized the American Economic Association in 1885, recruiting a host of other professors, who then made the association into a vehicle for promoting socialism.

Present at the founders' meeting was Thomas Davidson, an itinerant scholar, who had helped found the Fabian Society in London during the previous year.

In 1888 there appeared a book that was to give a tremendous boost to the socialist movement in America. It was a utopian fantasy written by a journalist, Edward Bellamy, entitled *Looking Backward*. It became a best seller and one of the most influential books of its time.

Looking Backward is the story of Julian West, a Bostonian, who falls asleep in 1887 and wakes in the year 2000 to find that a bloodless socialist revolution has taken place in America and that now the government owns everything through nationalization. The entire economy is organized around an Industrial Army, in which every citizen must serve from the age of twenty-one to forty-five. Everyone is paid equally, but not in money, for money has been abolished.

"A credit corresponding to his share of the annual product of the nation is given to every citizen on the public books at the beginning of each year, and a credit card is issued him with which he procures at the public storehouses whatever he desires." No buying or selling among private citizens is permitted, for "buying and selling is essentially antisocial in all its tendencies."

And, of course, in Bellamy's utopia, evil and crime have virtually disappeared. Bellamy wrote: "The Ten Commandments became well-nigh obsolete in a world where there was no temptation to theft, no occasion to lie either for fear or favor, no room for envy where all were equal, and little provocation to violence where men were disarmed of power to injure one another. Humanity's ancient dream of liberty, equality, fraternity ... at last was realized.... It was for the first time possible to see what unperverted human nature really was like.... Soon was fully realized, what the divines and philosophers of old would never have believed, that human nature in its essential qualities is good, not bad, that men by their natural intention and structure are generous, not selfish, pitiful, not cruel, sympathetic, not arrogant, godlike in aspirations, instinct with divinest impulses of tenderness and self-sacrifice, images of God indeed, not the travesties upon Him they had seemed." Paradise indeed had been achieved!

As ridiculous as all of this sounds today, Bellamy not only believed in what he wrote but considered it to be "a forecast, in accordance with the principles of evolution, of the next stage in the industrial and social development of humanity, especially in this country."

Countless Americans shared his belief. So great was their enthusiasm that they organized the Nationalist Club — nationalist standing for nationalization — a kind of American Fabian Society dedicated to promoting the principle of the "Brotherhood of Man" and the nationalization of private industry. Their credo stated:

> [T]hose who seek the welfare of man must endeavor to suppress the system founded on brute principles of competition and put in its place another based on the nobler principles of association.... We advocate no sudden or ill-considered changes; we make no war upon individuals who have accumulated immense for-

tunes simply by carrying to a logical end the false principles upon which business is now based.

The combinations, trusts and syndicates of which the people at present complain demonstrate the practicability of our basic principle of association. We merely seek to push this principle a little further and have all industries operated in the interests of the nation — the people organized — the organic unity of the whole people.

The aim of the Nationalist Club was to "educate" the American people through lectures, books, and publications in the general principles of economic reform advocated by Bellamy, which would eventually lead to the establishment of the cooperative commonwealth.

The movement grew rapidly, and by 1891 there were 165 Nationalist Clubs throughout the country. Particularly drawn to the movement were the followers of Theosophist occultists Annie Besant and Helena Blavatsky. Of *Looking Backward*, Blavatsky wrote in 1889 that it "admirably represents the Theosophical idea of what should be the first great step toward the full realization of universal brotherhood."

However, by 1893 most of the Nationalist Clubs had disappeared, with their hard-core socialist members becoming active in any number of educational enterprises. One of these enterprises was a new monthly journal which made its appearance in 1895, *The American Fabian*, published by the Fabian Educational Company of Boston. The editors wrote:

> We call our paper "The American Fabian" because our politics must in a measure differ from those of the English Fabians.... England's (unwritten) Constitution readily admits of constant though gradual modification. Our American Constitution does not readily admit of such change. England can thus move into Socialism almost imperceptibly. Our Constitution being largely individualistic must be changed to admit of Socialism, and each change necessitates a political crisis.

Thus by the 1890s it had become apparent to American socialists that the United States Constitution represented a formidable obstacle to the creation of a socialist America.

In April 1898, Sidney and Beatrice Webb arrived in the United States where they were wined and dined by the socialist elite. In Chicago the Webbs stayed at Hull House as guests of its legendary founder Jane Addams, pioneer in the settlement house movement.

It was probably at this time that John Dewey, then professor at the University of Chicago, met the Webbs. Dewey had close relations with Hull House, founded in 1889 by Addams. He was on its first board of trustees and even conducted courses there. According to biographer George Dykhuizen, "Dewey owed much to the influences he encountered at Hull House. His contact with people with more radical and extreme views than his deepened and sharpened his own."

Eventually Dewey was to become America's leading strategist for socialism, and it is obvious that he took his cue from the Fabians. How did Dewey become a socialist? The story is interesting.

John Dewey was born in Vermont in 1859 and was raised in a Christian family of Puritan heritage. He attended a liberal-leaning Congregational Church and taught Sunday school. In 1875 he entered the University of Vermont. Max Eastman wrote of a crisis in Dewey's junior year that marked a turning point in the young man's life:

> The crisis was a short course in physiology with a textbook written by Thomas Henry Huxley. That accidental contact with Darwin's brilliant disciple, then waging his fierce war for evolution against the impregnable rock of Holy Scripture, woke John Dewey up to the spectacular excitement of the effort to understand the world. He was swept off his feet by the rapture of scientific knowledge.

In 1881 Dewey began studies for his doctorate at Johns Hopkins University. There, encouraged by George Sylvester Morris, his professor, he became a Hegelian. The powerful attraction of Hegel's philosophy was that it permitted an individual to embrace science and evolution, discard the notion of sin, but still retain some notion of God. Eastman wrote:

> Hegel invented a most ingenious disguise, a truly wondrous scheme for keeping deity in the world....His scheme was,

in brief, to say that all reality, good and bad together, is the Divine Spirit in a process of inward, and also onward and upward, struggle toward the realization of its own free and complete being. Many years before natural science began to see the world as in process of evolution, Hegel was ready for them with his theory that God himself is a world in process of evolution. Nothing more prodigiously ingenious was ever invented by the mind of man than this Hegelian scheme for defending soulfulness against science.

It was also at Johns Hopkins that Dewey was introduced to the New Psychology by G. Stanley Hall, who had studied in Leipzig under Professor Wilhelm Wundt. Dewey took all of Hall's courses in experimental and physiological psychology.

In 1884, Dewey was brought to the University of Michigan as instructor in philosophy by Professor Morris, who was then head of the department. The two men, steeped in Hegelianism, enjoyed a rich personal and intellectual friendship. It was also at Michigan that Dewey met Alice Chapman, a strong-minded young lady from a family of radicals and freethinkers. Dewey fell in love, and they married in 1886. Dewey later told a friend, "No two people were ever more in love."

In 1887, Dewey published his textbook, *Psychology*, which was his fullest and most successful articulation of his Hegelian approach, blended with the new experimental psychology. In 1888, Dewey went to the University of Minnesota as head of the philosophy department. Most probably Dewey read *Looking Backward* in that year, because it was then that he also wrote his essay, "The Ethics of Democracy," in which he formulated a new collectivist concept for American democracy. He rejected the notion that America was made up of individuals who expressed their political will through a constitutionally established elective and legislative process. He claimed that such a notion inferred that men "in their natural state are non-social units, a mere multitude." On the contrary, he argued, society is organic and "the citizen is a member of the organism, and, just in proportion to the perception of the organism, has concentrated within himself its intelligence and will."

This was simply another way of phrasing Bellamy's concept of the nation, as described in *Looking Backward*, "not as an association of men for certain political functions affecting their happiness only remotely and superficially, but as a family, a vital union, a common life, a mighty heaven-touching tree, whose leaves are its people, fed from its veins, and feeding it in turn."

Dewey, in his essay, expanded on this organic concept: "But human society represents a more perfect organism. The whole lives truly in every member, and there is no longer the appearance of physical aggregation, or continuity. The organism manifests itself as what it truly is, an ideal or spiritual life, a unity of *will*.... In conception, at least, democracy approaches most nearly the ideal of all social organizations: that in which the individual and society are organic to each other."

And how did this organic and rather Platonic-Hegelian view of society affect individual liberty? Dewey wrote:

> Nothing could be more aside from the mark than to say that the Platonic ideal subordinates and sacrifices the individual to the state. It does, indeed, hold that the individual can be what he ought to be, can become what, in idea, he is, only as a member of a spiritual organism, called by Plato the state, and, in losing his own individual will, acquiring that of this larger reality. But this is not loss of selfhood or personality, it is its realization. The individual is not sacrificed; he is brought to reality in the state.

Now you see it, now you don't. Dewey was quite adept at this sort of intellectual shell game. He argued quite passionately that we had to stop looking at the individual in isolation.

> Liberty is not a numerical notion of isolation; it is the ethical idea that personality is the supreme and only law, that every man is an absolute end in himself ... but the chief stimuli and encouragements to the realization of personality come from society....
>
> Equality is not an arithmetical but an ethical conception.... Equality, in short, is the ideal of humanity; an ideal in the consciousness of which democracy lives and moves.... And there

is no need to beat about the bush in saying that democracy is not in reality what it is in name until it is industrial, as well as civil and political.

And finally Dewey wrapped it up with, "The idea of democracy, the ideas of liberty, equality, and fraternity, represent a society in which the distinction between the spiritual and secular has ceased ... the divine and the human organization of society are one."

These are the terms in which Dewey was to argue, in the years ahead, that in the democratic state God and man were one, a blend of Hegelian idealism, utopian fantasy, and Platonic logic. It was about as far as one could go from the ideology of the Founding Fathers without becoming a Marxist revolutionary or, in later years, a terrorist for Lenin.

Dewey's rejection of eighteenth century individualistic liberalism, with its notion of unalienable rights, was complete and irrevocable, and in time he was to remove God from his political equation, substituting humanism for religion. But his admiration for Edward Bellamy never waned. In 1934, in a tribute to Bellamy entitled "The Great American Prophet," he wrote that Bellamy was "imbued with a religious faith in the democratic ideal.... But what distinguishes Bellamy is that he grasped the human meaning of democracy as an idea of equality and liberty. No one has carried through the idea that equality is obtainable only by complete equality of income more fully than Bellamy."

In 1889, the untimely death of George Morris created a crisis at Michigan, and Dewey was brought back to head the philosophy department. He remained at Michigan until 1894. During his time there he was a member of the Congregational Church at Ann Arbor. Dykhuizen, his biographer, wrote:

> Because the Hegelianism of Morris and Dewey had a place for traditional Christian concepts, the extension of its point of view to the several courses in philosophy and psychology gave the department a distinctly religious atmosphere that satisfied all but the most orthodox that the religious faith of the students was as safe under Morris and Dewey as it had been under clergymen.

In 1894, Dewey left Michigan and joined the faculty at the University of Chicago as Chairman of the Department of Philosophy, Psychology, and Pedagogy. The new university, only four years old, and endowed by John D. Rockefeller, was directed by President William Rainey Harper, a theological liberal. By then Dewey had come to the conclusion that the only road to socialism in America was the long persevering one of education. That his aim was radical reform was made quite clear in an essay, written in 1894, entitled "Reconstruction":

> The radical, the one who is for progress, cannot gain his end if he shuts himself off from established facts of life. If he turns to the future before he has taken home to himself the meaning of the past, his efforts will in so far be futile.... It is folly, it is worse than folly, it is mere individual conceit, for one to set out to reform the world, either at large or in detail, until he has learned what the existing world which he wishes to reform has for him to learn.... The most progressive force in life is the idea of the past set free from its local and partial bonds and moving on to the fuller expression of its own destiny.

While the use of the word "destiny" gives evidence that Dewey was still strongly under the influence of Hegelian idealism, his views had undergone significant changes during the last years at Michigan. In fact, his formal connection with organized religion ended when he left Ann Arbor. A few years after settling in Chicago, he withdrew his membership from the church in Ann Arbor and did not ask for a letter of transferral to a church in Chicago. He had by then become a pragmatic materialist, having shed the Hegelian concept of the Absolute and adopted a more comfortable concept of moral relativism.

It was now as Chairman of the Department of Pedagogy that Dewey began to concentrate his efforts on education. Dewey realized that if the scenario in Bellamy's *Looking Backward* was ever to be realized, it would have to be done by preparing the young not only to accept a socialist way of life but to want to bring it about. The situation at Chicago afforded Dewey the opportunity to put his educational ideas into practice by creating an experimental school. The school would serve as a laboratory for psychology and pedagogy in the same manner that labs were used for experiments in the physical sciences. In fact, it came to be known as the Laboratory School.

The purpose of the school was to find out what kind of curriculum was needed to create that social individual who would fit easily into a socialist society. The question for the radical educator was how to socialize children so that they became the kind of selfless egalitarians who would serve the organic state as willingly and uncomplainingly as the citizens of Bellamy's utopia and would work assiduously to create such a utopia.

Dewey decided that the best way to achieve this new collectivist personality was to turn the classroom into a place where these desirable social traits could be developed. He wrote:

> Since the integration of the individual and the social is impossible except when the individual lives in close association with others in the constant free give and take of experiences, it seemed that education could prepare the young for the future social life only when the school was itself a cooperative society on a small scale.

What kind of curriculum would fit a school that was a mini-cooperative society? Dewey's recommendation was indeed radical: build the curriculum not around academic subjects but occupational activities that provided maximum opportunities for socialization.

Since the beginning of Western civilization, the school curriculum centered around the development of academic skills, the intellectual faculties, and high literacy. Now Dewey wanted to change all of that. Why? Because high literacy produced that abominable form of individualism which was basically, as Dewey believed, anti-social. From Dewey's point of view, the school's primary commitment to literacy was indeed the key to the whole problem.

In 1898 he wrote an essay, "The Primary-Education Fetich," in which he explained exactly what he meant:

> There is ... a false educational god whose idolators are legion, and whose cult influences the entire educational system. This is language study — the study not of foreign language, but of

English; not in higher, but in primary education. It is almost an unquestioned assumption, of educational theory and practice both, that the first three years of a child's school life shall be mainly taken up with learning to read and write his own language. If we add to this the learning of a certain amount of numerical combinations, we have the pivot about which primary education swings....

It does not follow, however, that because this course was once wise it is so any longer.... The present has its claims. It is in education, if anywhere, that the claims of the present should be controlling.... My proposition is, that conditions — social, industrial, and intellectual — have undergone such a radical change, that the time has come for a thoroughgoing examination of the emphasis put upon linguistic work in elementary instruction....

The plea for the predominance of learning to read in early school life because of the great importance attaching to literature seems to me a perversion.

Dewey then argued how important it was for the child to experience life through classroom activities, projects, and social interaction before learning to read about them. And the reading materials themselves had to be relevant to the child's needs. He wrote:

Every respectable authority insists that the period of childhood, lying between the years of four and eight or nine, is the plastic period in sense and emotional life. What are we doing to shape these capacities? What are we doing to feed this hunger? If one compared the powers and needs of the child in these directions with what is actually supplied in the regimen of the three R's, the contrast is pitiful and tragic.... No one can clearly set before himself the vivacity and persistency of the child's motor instincts at this period, and then call to mind the continued grind of reading and writing, without feeling that the justification of our present curriculum is psychologically impossible. It is simply superstition: it is a remnant of an outgrown period of history.

Finally, Dewey, the master strategist, set forth what must be done:

Change must come gradually. To force it unduly would compromise its final success by favoring a violent reaction. What is needed in the first place, is that there should be a full and frank statement of conviction with regard to the matter from physiologists and psychologists and from those school administrators who are conscious of the evils of the present regime.... Wherever movements looking to a solution of the problem are intelligently undertaken, they should receive encouragement, moral and financial, from the intellectual leaders of the community. There are already in existence a considerable number of educational "experimental stations," which represent the outposts of educational progress. If these schools can be adequately supported for a number of years they will perform a great vicarious service. After such schools have worked out carefully and definitely the subject matter of a new curriculum — finding the right place for language-studies and placing them in their right perspective — the problem of the more general educational reform will be immensely simplified and facilitated.

Here was, indeed, a master plan, involving the entire progressive educational community, to create a new socialist curriculum for the schools of America, a plan that was indeed carried out and implemented. However, it was in Dewey's famous statement of belief, "My Pedagogic Creed," written in 1897, that he spelled out quite clearly that the school was to be the vehicle of America's socialist revolution. Again he put forth his collectivist concepts of an organic society, the social individual, the downgrading of academics, and the need to use psychology in education. He wrote:

I believe that all education proceeds by the participation of the individual in the social consciousness of the race.... He becomes an inheritor of the funded capital of civilization.... Without insight into the psychological structure and activities of the individual, the education process will be haphazard and arbitrary.... In sum, I believe that the individual who is to be educated is a social individual and that society is an organic union of individuals.

I believe that the school is primarily a social institution. Education being a social process, the school is simply a form of community life in which all those agencies are concentrated that will be most effective in bringing the child to share in the inherited resources of the race, and to use his own powers for social ends.

I believe that education, therefore, is a process of living and not a preparation for future living.

It is true that language is a logical instrument, but it is fundamentally and primarily a social instrument.

I believe that the image is the great instrument of instruction.

I believe that much of the time and attention now given to the preparation and presentation of lessons might be more wisely and profitably expended in training the child's power of imagery and in seeing to it that he was continually forming definite, vivid, and growing images of the various subjects with which he comes in contact in his experience.

I believe that education is the fundamental method of social progress and reform.

I believe that all reforms which rest simply upon the enactment of law, or the threatening of certain penalties, or upon changes in mechanical or outward arrangements, are transitory and futile.

I believe that education is the regulation of the process of coming to share in the social consciousness; and that adjustment of individual activity on the basis of this social consciousness is the only sure method of social reconstruction....

I believe it is the business of every one interested in education to insist upon the school as the primary and most effective interest of social progress and reform in order that society may be awakened to realize what the school stands for, and aroused to the necessity of endowing the educator with sufficient equipment properly to perform his task....

I believe that with the growth of psychological science, ... and with the growth of social science ... all scientific resources can be utilized for the purposes of education....

I believe that every teacher ... is a social servant set apart for the maintenance of proper social order and the securing of the right social growth.

I believe that in this way the teacher always is the prophet of the true God and the usherer in of the true kingdom of God.

You couldn't get any more messianic than that! It was the intensity of Dewey's ideological commitment that made him the philosophical leader of the American socialist revolution. He formulated its basic strategy of revolution via education.

One hundred years have gone by since Dewey set American education on its progressive course. The result is an education system in shambles, a rising national tide of illiteracy and the social misery caused in its wake. Bellamy's vision of a socialist utopia in the year 2000 is even more remote today than it was in 1888. In England the Fabian tortoise has been quashed by Margaret Thatcher, and in America orthodox religion, once considered quite extinct, is growing in strength and influence, creating waves of pessimism among secular humanists. The worldwide disillusionment with socialism is so great that even the Soviet Union has given up the experiment and returned to normal political development.

In 1899 Dewey published *School and Society*, his blueprint for socialism via education. It clearly established him as the leader of progressive education. In 1904 he left Chicago and joined the faculty at Columbia University and Teachers College in New York. There he grew in stature as the moral interpreter of American progressivism.

The reason why Dewey comes across as so distinctly American is because he took his socialist vision from Bellamy, not Marx. And yet the society in the world today that comes closest to Bellamy' s vision is Castro's Cuba. Meanwhile, we in the United States must live with the disastrous consequences of the Dewey-inspired curriculum.

LOOKING BACKWARD
100 YEARS LATER

The year 1988 marked the 100th anniversary of the publication of Edward Bellamy's famous utopian novel, *Looking Backward*, in which the author depicted a happy, socialist America in the year 2000. In Bellamy's optimistic fantasy, greed and material want ceased to exist, brotherly harmony prevailed, the arts and sciences flourished, and an all-powerful and pervasive government and bureaucracy were efficient and fair.

The book became enormously popular, selling 371,000 copies in its first two years and a million copies by 1900. Its influence on American progressive educators and intellectuals was enormous. In fact, it became their vision of a future American paradise in which human moral perfectibility could at last be attained. The extent of the book's influence can be measured by the fact that in 1935, when Columbia University asked philosopher-educator John Dewey, historian Charles Beard, and *Atlantic Monthly* editor Edward Weeks to prepare independently lists of the twenty-five most influential books since 1885, *Looking Backward* ranked as second on each list after Marx's *Das Kapital*. In other words, *Looking Backward* was considered the most influential American book in that fifty-year period.

John Dewey characterized the book as "one of the greatest modern syntheses of humane values." Even after the rise of Hitler's National Socialism in Germany and Marxist-Leninist-Stalinist communism in Russia, Dewey still clung to Bellamy's vision of a socialist America. In his 1934 essay, "The Great American Prophet," Dewey wrote:

> I wish that those who conceive that the abolition of private capital and of energy expended for profit signify complete regimenting of life and the abolition also of all personal choice and all emulation, would read with an open mind Bellamy's

picture of a socialized economy. It is not merely that he exposes with vigor and clarity the restriction upon liberty that the present system imposes but that he pictures how socialized industry and finance would release and further all of those personal and private types of occupation and use of leisure that men and women actually most prize today....

It is an American communism that he depicts, and his appeal comes largely from the fact that he sees in it the necessary means of realizing the democratic ideal....

The worth of Bellamy's books in effecting a translation of the ideas of democracy into economic terms is incalculable. What *Uncle Tom's Cabin* was to the anti-slavery movement, Bellamy's book may well be to the shaping of popular opinion for a new social order.

Bellamy envisaged America becoming socialist by way of consensus rather than revolution. In turn, Dewey, who spent his professional life trying to transform American reality into Bellamy's vision, saw education as the principal means by which this transformation could be realized. He spent the years 1894 to 1904 at the University of Chicago in his Laboratory School seeking to devise a new curriculum for the public schools that would produce the kind of socialized youngsters who would bring about the new socialist millennium. The result, of course, is the education we have today — a minimal interest in the development of intellectual skills and a maximal effort to produce socialized behavior.

Today, many years later, the University of Chicago stands as an island of academic tranquility in Chicago's Southside, surrounded by a sea of social and urban devastation caused by the philosophical emanations from Dewey's laboratory and other departments. Charles Judd, the university's Wundtian professor of educational psychology, labored mightily to organize the radical reform of the public school curriculum to conform with Dewey's plan.

According to Dewey, the philosophical underpinning of capitalism was individualism, sustained by an education that stressed the development of literacy skills. High literacy encouraged intellectual independence, which produced strong individualism. It was Dewey's exhaustive analysis of individualism that led him to believe the socialized individual could only be produced by first getting rid of the traditional emphasis on language and literacy and instead turning the children toward socialized activities and behavior. In 1898 he wrote a devastating critique of three R's education, entitled "The Primary-Education Fetich," in which he took to task the entire traditional emphasis on literacy. He wrote: "The plea for the predominance of learning to read in early school life because of the great importance attaching to literature seems to me a perversion."

And then he mapped out a long-range, comprehensive strategy that would reorganize primary education to serve the needs of socialization. "Change must come gradually," he wrote. "To force it unduly would compromise its final success by favoring a violent reaction."

Obviously, Dewey had learned a lot from Fabian socialists whose motto was *Festina lente* — "Make haste slowly."

Part of the new primary curriculum was a new ideographic method of teaching reading — the look-say or sight method. In fact, it was at the University of Chicago that Charles Judd's protégé, William Scott Gray, developed the Dick and Jane reading program which in the 1930s became the standard method of teaching reading in American schools and has caused the devastating epidemic of functional illiteracy in America.

False doctrines lead to tragic consequences. Chicago's Southside, New York's Harlem and East Bronx, Boston's Roxbury, and other such third-world enclaves in American cities, peopled by the new American underclass, all of whom have attended American public schools, are the consequences of the arrogant, eugenicist doctrines, policies, and strategies of the progressive movement. Progressives, of course, will never admit responsibility for what they have wrought. In fact, they have deified Dewey, attributing the failures of progressive education to faulty implementation of Dewey's ideas.

Meanwhile, Bellamy's utopia is far more remote today than it was in 1888. The twentieth century, with its moral and political diseases, its holocausts, its pagan perversions, has made the delusion of

human perfectibility a tragic joke. Today we know that Bellamy's —
as well as Dewey's — basic analysis of capitalism and human nature
was false. Their ridiculous ideas have come crashing down around us.
But the educators haven't noticed, thus once more affirming Calvin's
brilliant insight into man's total depravity. Blasphemous, disobedient
man has feasted off the tree of the knowledge of good and evil, and
still can't tell the difference! After all, to play God is the ultimate self-
deception.

WHO KILLED EXCELLENCE?

The history of American education can be roughly divided into three distinct periods, each representing a particular and powerful worldview. The first period — from colonial times to the 1840s — saw the dominance of the Calvinist ethic: God's omnipotent sovereignty was the central reality of man's existence. In the Calvinist scheme, the purpose of man's life was to glorify God, and the attainment of Biblical literacy was considered the overriding spiritual and moral function of education. Latin, Greek, and Hebrew were studied because they were the original languages of the Bible and of theological literature. Thus this period in American education is characterized by a very high standard of literacy.

The second period, lasting from the 1840s until about World War I, reflects the Hegelian mindset. W. F. Hegel's statist-idealist philosophy spread throughout the Western world like a malignant spiritual disease, destroying Calvinism. In this pantheistic scheme, the purpose of life was to glorify man and the instrument through which man's collective power could be exercised — the state. Hegel dethroned the Jehovah of the Old Testament and the Christ of the New Testament, and offered a pantheistic view of the universe where everything was a somewhat formless "god" in the process of perfecting himself through a dynamic, endless struggle called the dialectic. Yet even the Hegelian period was one of high literacy, for Hegel had stressed intellectual development, since he considered man's mind to be the highest manifestation of God in the universe. Latin and Greek were studied because they were the languages of the pagan classics.

During this Hegelian period the public school movement developed, promoting a secular form of education that gradually eliminated the Bible from the classrooms of America. Discipline, punctuality, high academic standards and achievement were the hallmarks of the public schools.

The third period, from World War I to the present, I call "progressive." It came into being mainly as a result of the new behavioral psychology developed in the experimental laboratories of Wilhelm Wundt at the University of Leipzig in Germany. The major American figures who studied under Wundt — James McKeen Cattell, G. Stanley Hall, Charles H. Judd, and James Earl Russell — came back to the United States to revolutionize American education.

In this scheme, the purpose of man's life was to deny and reject the supernatural and to sacrifice oneself to the collective, often referred to as "humanity." Science and evolution replaced religion as the focus of faith, and dialectical materialism superseded Hegel's dialectical idealism as the process by which man's moral progress was made. The word "progressive," in fact, comes from this dialectical concept of progress.

G. Stanley Hall beat the first path to Wundt's laboratory in Leipzig. Hall had already spent the years 1868–1870 studying in Germany and had returned home seething with hatred for his Puritan New England heritage. He wrote in his autobiography:

> I fairly loathed and hated so much that I saw about me that I now realize more clearly than ever how possible it would have been for me to have drifted into some, perhaps almost any, camp of radicals and to have come into such open rupture with the scheme of things as they were that I should have been stigmatized as dangerous, at least for any academic career, where the motto was Safety First. And as this was the only way left open, the alternative being the dread one of going back to the farm, it was most fortunate that these deeply stirred instincts of revolt were never openly expressed and my rank heresies and socialist leanings unknown.

Hall returned from his Wundtian experience in 1878 and in 1882 created America's first psychology laboratory at Johns Hopkins University. Two of Hall's students were James McKeen Cattell and John Dewey. Cattell journeyed to Leipzig in 1884 where he spent two years studying under Professor Wundt. He returned to the U.S. and created the world's first psychology department at the University of Pennsylvania in 1887. One biographical account of Cattell's life states:

Cattell's student years in Baltimore, Germany, and England — the period of his greatest originality and productivity in psychology — were laced with inner complaint. Cattell confided only in his private journal his recurrent feelings of depression, his frequent need of hallucinogenic drugs, and his underlying philosophic stance as a "skeptic and mystic."

Is it not interesting that hallucinogenic drugs were already being used by students of psychology as far back as the 1880s? In 1891 Cattell established Columbia University's department of psychology. During his years at Columbia, Cattell trained more future members of the American Psychological Association than did any other institution. Indeed, Cattell was one of the founders of the American Psychological Association and the *Psychological Review*. Under his direction, psychology at Columbia became one of the strongest departments of research and advanced teaching.

No doubt Cattell's most celebrated pupil was Edward L. Thorndike, who had gotten his master's degree under William James at Harvard, where he had also conducted experiments in animal learning. Under Cattell, Thorndike continued his experiments that were to have a devastating impact on American education.

Thorndike reduced psychology to the study of observable, measurable human behavior — with the complexity and mystery of mind and soul left out. In summing up his theory of learning, Thorndike wrote: "The best way with children may often be, in the pompous words of an animal trainer, 'to arrange everything in connection with the trick so that the animal will be compelled by the laws of its own nature to perform it.'"

In 1904, Cattell invited his old friend John Dewey to join the faculty at Columbia. From Johns Hopkins, Dewey had not gone to Leipzig like Cattell and others. Instead he taught philosophy at the University of Michigan for about nine years. He had left Johns Hopkins a Hegelian idealist but became a materialist at Michigan. In 1894 he became professor of philosophy and education at the University of Chicago where he created his famous Laboratory School.

The purpose of the school was to see what kind of curriculum was needed to produce socialists instead of capitalists, collectivists instead of individualists. Dewey, along with the other adherents of the new psychology, was convinced that socialism was the wave of the future and that individualism was passé. But the individualist system would not fade away on its own as long as it was sustained by the education American children were getting in their schools. According to Dewey, "[E]ducation is growth under favorable conditions; the school is the place where those conditions should be regulated scientifically."

In other words, if we apply psychology to education, which we have done now for over fifty years, then the ideal classroom is a psych lab and the pupils within it are laboratory animals.

Dewey's joining Cattell and Thorndike at Columbia brought together the lethal trio who were literally to wipe out our traditional education and kill academic excellence in America. It would not be accomplished overnight, for an army of new teachers and superintendents had to be trained and an army of old teachers and superintendents had to retire or die off.

By 1908 the trio had produced three books of paramount importance to the progressive movement. Thorndike published *Animal Intelligence* in 1898; Dewey published *School and Society* in 1899; and in 1908, Cattell produced, through a surrogate by the name of Edmund Burke Huey, *The Psychology and Pedagogy of Reading.*

Dewey provided the social philosophy of the movement, Thorndike the teaching theories and techniques, and Cattell the organizing energy. There was among all of them, disciples and colleagues, a missionary zeal to rebuild American education on a foundation of science, evolution, humanism, and behaviorism. But it was Dewey who identified high literacy as the culprit in traditional education, the sustaining force behind individualism. He wrote in 1898:

> My proposition is, that conditions — social, industrial, and intellectual — have undergone such a radical change, that the time has come for a thoroughgoing examination of the emphasis put upon linguistic work in elementary instruction....
>
> The plea for the predominance of learning to read in early school-life because of the great importance attaching to literature seems to me a perversion.

But in order to reform the system, the mind had to be seen in a different way. Dewey wrote:

> The idea of heredity has made familiar the notion that the equipment of the individual, mental as well as physical, is an inheritance from the race: a capital inherited by the individual from the past and held in trust by him for the future. The idea of evolution has made familiar the notion that the mind cannot be regarded as an individual, monopolistic possession, but represents the outworkings of the endeavor and thought of humanity.

To Dewey the one part of our identity that is the most private, the mind, is really not the property of the individual at all, but of humanity, which is merely a euphemism for the collective or the state. That concept is at the very heart of the Orwellian nightmare, and yet the same concept is the very basis of our progressive-humanist-behaviorist education system.

Dewey realized that such radical reform was not exactly what the American people wanted. So he wrote: "Change must come gradually. To force it unduly would compromise its final success by favoring a violent reaction."

The most important of the reforms to be instituted was changing the way children were to be taught to read. Since it had been ordained by Dewey and his colleagues that literacy skills were to be drastically deemphasized in favor of the development of social skills, a new teaching method that deliberately reduced literacy skills was needed.

The traditional school used the phonics or phonetic method. That is, children were first taught the alphabet, then the sounds the letters stand for, and in a short time they became independent readers. The new method — look-say or the word method — taught children to read English as if it were Chinese or Egyptian hieroglyphics.

The new method had been invented in the 1830s by Rev. Thomas H. Gallaudet, the famous teacher of the deaf and dumb. Since deaf-mutes have no conception of a spoken language, they could not hear a phonetic — or sound-symbol— system of reading.

Instead, they were taught to read by a purely sight method consisting of pictures juxtaposed with whole words. Thus, the whole word was seen to represent an idea or image, not the sounds of language. The written word itself was regarded as a little picture, much like a Chinese ideograph. Gallaudet thought that the method could be adapted for use by normal children, and he wrote a little primer on that concept.

In 1837 the Boston Primary School Committee decided to adopt the primer. By 1844 the results were so disastrous that a group of Boston schoolmasters published a blistering attack on the whole-word method, and it was thrown out of the schools. But look-say was kept alive in the new state normal schools where it was taught as a legitimate alternative to the alphabetic-phonics method.

When the progressives decided to revive look-say, they realized that an authoritative book would be necessary to give the new method the seal of approval of the new psychology. In Wundt's laboratory, Cattell had observed that adults could read whole words just as fast as they could read individual letters. From that he concluded that a child could be taught to read simply by showing him whole words and telling him what they said.

For some reason, Cattell did not want to write a book himself. So he got one of G. Stanley Hall's students, Edmund Burke Huey, to write a book arguing that look-say was the superior way to teach reading. The book, *The Psychology and Pedagogy of Reading*, was published in 1908. What is astounding is that by 1908 Cattell and his colleagues were very well aware that the look-say method produced inaccurate readers. In fact, Huey argued in favor of inaccuracy as a virtue!

The book was immediately adopted by the progressives as the authoritative work on the subject despite the fact that it was written by an obscure student who had had no experience whatever in the teaching of reading, who wrote nothing further on the subject, and about whom virtually nothing is known.

When a nation's leading educational reformers start arguing in favor of illiteracy and inaccurate reading, and damning early emphasis on learning to read as a perversion, then we can expect some strange results to come from our education process. In fact, by the 1950s, the progressives had done such a good job that Rudolf Flesch could write a book in 1955 entitled *Why Johnny Can't Read*. Why indeed! Flesch minced no words: "The teaching of reading — all over the United States, in all the schools, in all the textbooks — is totally wrong and flies in the face of all logic and common sense."

How did this happen? Flesch explained:

> It's a foolproof system all right. Every gradeschool teacher in the country has to go to a teachers' college or school of education; every teachers' college gives at least one course on how to teach reading; every course on how to teach reading is based on a textbook; every one of those textbooks is written by one of the high priests of the word method. In the old days it was impossible to keep a good teacher from following her own common sense and practical knowledge; today the phonetic system of teaching reading is kept out of our schools as effectively as if we had a dictatorship with an all-powerful Ministry of Education.

The educators were furious with Flesch. He had made them appear stupid and incompetent. They knew they were not stupid. They had pulled off the greatest conspiracy against intelligence in history. Although Dewey, Thorndike, and Cattell were dead, their disciples, Arthur I. Gates at Columbia and William Scott Gray at the University of Chicago, were determined to carry on the work of their mentors.

In 1955, the professors of reading organized the International Reading Association to maintain the dominance of look-say in primary reading instruction. Today, look-say permeates the educational marketplace so thoroughly and in so many guises, and it is so widely and uncritically accepted, that it takes expert knowledge by a teacher or parent to know the good from the bad, the useful from the harmful.

Even the best students have fallen victim to this "dumbing-down" process. In a speech given to the California Library Association in 1970, Karl Shapiro, the eminent poet-professor who had taught creative writing for over twenty years, told his audience:

What is really distressing is that this generation cannot and does not read. I am speaking of university students in what are supposed to be our best universities. Their illiteracy is staggering.... We are experiencing a literacy breakdown which is unlike anything I know of in the history of letters.

This literacy breakdown is no accident. It is not the result of ignorance or incompetence. It has been, in fact, deliberately created by our progressive-humanistic behaviorist educators whose social agenda is far more important to them than anything connected with academic excellence. Perhaps their mindset was best expressed by psychologist Arthur W. Combs in an essay entitled "Humanistic Goals of Education," published in 1975. Dr. Combs wrote:

Modern education must produce far more than persons with cognitive skills. It must produce *humane* individuals.... The humane qualities are absolutely essential to our way of life — far more important, even, than the learning of reading, for example. We can live with a bad reader; a bigot is a danger to everyone.

The inference, of course, it that you can't have both good readers and humane persons, that one must be sacrificed for the other. Note also the very subtle suggestion that high literacy may even produce bigotry. If this is what the humanists believe, then how can we expect them to promote high literacy?

In 1935 Dewey wrote: "The last stand of oligarchical and anti-social seclusion is perpetuation of this purely individualistic notion of intelligence."

To kill this individualistic intelligence, which is the source of excellence, Dewey and his behaviorist colleagues proceeded to strip education of mind, soul, and literacy. In 1930 the percentage of illiteracy among white persons of native birth was 1.5. Among foreign-born whites it was 9.9 percent, and among Negroes it was 16.3. Among urban blacks the illiteracy rate was 9.2.

In 1935 a survey was made of Civilian Conservation Corps (CCC) enrollees. Of the 375,000 men studied, 1.9 percent were found to be illiterate, that is, they could not read a newspaper or write a letter. That's a remarkably low rate of illiteracy considering that most of the men who joined the CCC were in the low socio-economic group.

Today the illiteracy rate among urban blacks is probably about 40 percent, while the illiteracy rate among whites has been estimated to be from 7 to 30 percent. No one really knows the exact figure, including the Department of Education, which has guessed that there are about twenty-three million functional illiterates in America.

In fact, Dr. Flesch wrote another book in 1981 entitled *Why Johnny Still Can't Read*. He wrote with some sadness: "Twenty-five years ago I studied American methods of teaching reading and warned against educational catastrophe. Now it has happened."

At the moment, every state legislature in the nation is grappling with an education reform bill. Not one of them has addressed this basic problem of primary reading instruction. The trouble is that most would-be reformers are convinced that merit pay, longer school days, smaller class size, more homework, career ladders, competency tests, higher pay for teachers, compulsory kindergarten, and more preschool facilities will give us excellence. But they won't for one very significant reason. The academic substance of public education today is controlled lock, stock, and barrel by behavioral psychologists, and they don't believe in excellence. The American classroom has been transformed into a psych lab and the function of a psych lab is not academic excellence.

If education consists of the interaction between an effective teacher and a willing learner, then you can't have it in a psych lab that has neither. In the lab you have the trainer and the trainee, the controller and the controlled, the experimenter and the subject, the therapist and the patient. What should go on in a classroom is teaching and learning. What goes on in the psych lab is stimulus and response, diagnosis and treatment.

Many people think that behaviorism is simply the study of behavior. But according to B. F. Skinner, behaviorism is a theory of knowledge, in which knowing and thinking are regarded merely as forms of behavior. Although psychology was supposed to be the study of the life of the psyche — the mind — behaviorists, starting with Thorndike, reduced the functions of the mind to where today the mind ceases to be a factor in education. Behavioral objectives are the goals of today's teachers.

Who killed excellence? Behavioral psychology did. Why? Because it is based on a lie: that man is an animal, without mind or soul, and can be taught as an animal. And that concept is based on an even greater lie: that there is no God, no Creator.

And so the future of American education rests on the resolution of profoundly philosophical questions. Apparently no compromise between the ruling behaviorists and the rebellious fundamentalists is possible. As long as the progressive-humanist-behaviorists control the graduate schools of education and psychology, the professional organizations and journals, and the processes whereby curricula are developed and textbooks written and published, there is little possibility that public education can achieve academic excellence.

There is a growing belief that the solution lies in abandoning government education and transferring our energies and resources to the private sector, thereby expanding educational freedom, opportunity, and entrepreneurship. The American people want better education. They ought to be able to get it. But to do so, they will have to sweep away whatever obstacles to excellence the educators have erected. In fact, that is the problem — how to break down, overcome, or circumvent the obstacles to excellence.

The exodus of children from public schools is an indication that this is already happening. But the millions of children who remain in the government schools are at risk, in danger of becoming the functional illiterates, the underclass of tomorrow. Can we save them? We have the knowledge to do so. But do we have the will? The next few years will provide the answer.

CREATING DYSLEXIA: IT'S AS EASY AS PIE

few years ago, I had a demonstration of how easy it is to turn a perfectly normal child into a budding dyslexic. A father, in his early forties, brought his five-year-old kindergartner to me for an evaluation. The boy had had ear infections which the parents thought might interfere with his learning to read. He had some difficulty distinguishing *m*'s from *n*'s and his teacher said that the boy "wasn't catching on." Previously, the parents had signed a statement that they would make sure that the child did the homework assigned by the teacher.

The boy's pediatrician recommended that the child be core evaluated. At a core evaluation, teachers, counselors, and psychologists discuss what's wrong with the child with the parents. Then they recommend an individualized learning program. The father had heard about me and wanted my advice about the need or desirability of a core evaluation. Having served as a teacher in a private school for children with learning and behavioral problems, I had taken part in several core evaluations and was familiar with the process. But I wanted to meet the child and judge for myself whether or not he needed any kind of core evaluation.

The five-year-old turned out to be very friendly and from all appearances perfectly normal. First, I wanted to see if he could learn to read by intensive phonics. He was able to recite the alphabet, but he had not yet learned the letter sounds, and his ability to identify all of the letters correctly required more work on his part. This was quite normal for a five-year-old.

But I wanted to demonstrate to his father that the boy was quite capable of learning to read by phonics. So I turned to Lesson One in my *Alpha-Phonics* book, and I explained to the youngster that the letter *a* stood for the short *a* sound, which I then articulated quite distinctly. I asked the boy to repeat the sound, which he did. Then I pointed to the letter *m* and told the boy that the letter *m* stood for the "mmm" sound. And the boy was able to repeat the "mmm" with no problem. I then demonstrated that when we put the short "a" together with the "mmm" we get the word *am*.

I then introduced the letter *n* and its sound, "nnn." The boy repeated the sound quite nicely. I then joined the short "a" with the "nnn" to create the word *an*. The boy repeated the word. I told him that *an* was a word and asked him if he had ever used it. He said no. So I told him to listen to me, and I said, "I have *an* apple." He got the message. Meanwhile, through all of this he sat on his dad's lap and was smiling happily. I went through the rest of the consonants in the lesson: *s*, *t*, and *x*, showed how the words *as*, *at*, and *ax* were composed of two sounds, articulated the sounds, had him repeat them and demonstrated their use in short sentences. I asked him if he knew what an ax was. He did.

The purpose of the lesson was to show the father that his son was quite capable of learning to read by phonics, emphasizing that it would have to be done with much patience and repetition. Repetition and the use of flashcards were needed to produce automaticity. I did not think that the boy's hearing problem was even a problem. I was sure that his pronunciations would improve as he learned to read phonetically and that his very minor problem with *m* and *n* would clear up as he became a reader.

The father then showed me the papers his son had brought home from school. The math papers were simple counting exercises. There was also an exercise in categorizing. One exercise, which was supposed to test the youngster's ability to follow instructions, was somewhat confusing and got the child a failing grade in the exercise. That upset the father.

But what really perked my interest was the Dolch list of basic sight words that the child was supposed to memorize. The teacher had given the child this list of ninety words that were supposed to be memorized with the help of the parent — five words per week, from January to June. The first week's words were: *a, the, yellow, black, zero*. Second week's words: *and, away, big, blue, can*. Third week:

come, down, find, for, funny. Fourth week: *go, help, here, I, in.* And so on. Now, the child had hardly learned the alphabet and was not aware that letters stand for sounds. So why was he being given this arbitrary list of words to memorize by sight? Most of the words were perfectly regular in spelling and could have easily been learned in the context of a phonics reading program.

E. W. Dolch was a professor of education in the early 1920s who composed a list of the most frequently used words in English. It was thought that if children learned several hundred of these words by sight, that is, by whole-word recognition, before they even knew the alphabet or the letter sounds, they would have a jumping head start in learning to read. But what Dolch didn't realize is that once the child began automatically to look at English printed words as whole configurations, like Chinese characters, the child would develop a holistic reflex or habit that would then become a block against seeing our alphabetic words in their phonetic structure. And that block would cause the symptoms of what is known as dyslexia.

You might ask, what is a reflex? A reflex is a quick, automatic, habitual response to stimuli. There are two sorts of reflexes: unlearned (unconditioned) and learned (conditioned). An unlearned reflex is innately physical, such as the automatic reaction of our eyes when we enter a dark tunnel. The response is automatic and thus unlearned. A learned reflex is the kind we develop through habitual use, for example, in learning to drive. When we see a red light ahead, we automatically apply our foot to the brake pedal. We do this without thinking, while in the middle of a conversation or listening to the radio. That's a learned reflex. A learned reflex is not easy to unlearn. For example, an American who rents a car in England, where drivers drive on the left side of the road, must suppress his right-drive reflex if he is to avoid a head-on collision. In that case, the American driver can no longer rely on his normal reflexes and must think about every move he makes while driving.

That learning to read involved the development of conditioned reflexes was well-known by the professors of reading, especially when teaching a child to read by the sight method. Professor Walter Dearborn of Harvard University, wrote in 1940:

The principle which we have used to explain the acquisition of a sight vocabulary is, of course, the one suggested by Pavlov's well-known experiments on the conditioned response. This is as it should be. The basic process involved in conditioning and in learning to read is the same.

In order to obtain the best results from the use of the conditioning technique, the substitute stimulus must either immediately precede, or occur simultaneously with, the adequate stimulus. As we have explained before, the substitute stimulus in the case of learning to read is the word seen and the adequate stimulus is the word heard. (*School and Society*, 10/19/40, p. 368)

And so it was well-understood by the professors of reading that in learning to read, it was necessary to develop automaticity, a reflex. But the correct reflex to develop is a phonetic reflex, which is acquired by learning the letter sounds and being drilled sufficiently in the consonant-vowel combinations, so that the child learns to see the phonetic structure of a word and can automatically sound out the word by articulating each syllabic unit. In other words, the child automatically associates the letters with sounds. When that phonetic reflex is developed, reading becomes easy, fluent, and enjoyable.

But the development of a holistic reflex, as described by Professor Dearborn, creates an obstacle to the development of a phonetic reflex. It is this conflict, or collision, of reflexes that causes dyslexia. Undoubtedly, the professors of reading were well-aware that this conflict would develop, for they were acquainted with Pavlov's experiments in artificially creating behavioral disorganization by creating a conflict of reflexes. All of this was well expounded in a book written by one of Pavlov's colleagues, Alexander Luria, *The Nature of Human Conflicts, Researches in Disorganisation and Control of Human Behavior*, published in 1932. It had been translated from the Russian by W. Horsley Gantt, an American psychologist who had spent the years 1922 to 1929 working in Professor Pavlov's laboratories in the Soviet Union. In his preface to the book, Dr. Luria wrote:

The researches described here are the results of the experimental psychological investigations at the State Institute of Experimental Psychology, Moscow, during the period of 1923–1930. The chief problems of the author were an objective and materialistic description of the mechanisms lying at the basis of the disorganisation of human behaviour and an experimental approach to the laws of its regulation.... To accomplish this it was necessary to create artificially affects and models of experimental neuroses which made possible an analysis of the laws lying at the basis of the disintegration of behaviour. (p. xi)

In describing the results of the experiments, Luria wrote:

Pavlov obtained very definite affective "breaks," an acute disorganisation of behaviour, each time that the conditioned reflexes collided, when the animal was unable to react to two mutually exclusive tendencies, or was incapable of adequately responding to any imperative problem. (p. 12)

Luria wrote further:

We are not the first of those who have artificially created disorganisation of human behaviour. A large number of facts pertaining to this problem has been contributed by contemporary physiologists, as well as by psychologists.

I. P. Pavlov was the first investigator who, with the help of exceedingly bold workers, succeeded experimentally in creating neuroses with experimental animals. Working with conditioned reflexes in dogs, Pavlov came to the conclusion that every time an elaborated reflex came into conflict with the unconditioned reflex, the behaviour of the dog markedly changed....

Although, in the experiments with the collision of the conditioned reflexes in animals, it is fairly easy to obtain acute forms of artificial affect; it is much more difficult to get those results in human experiments.

The most successful attempts to produce experimental conflict psychologically are seen in the experiments of M. Ach. He formed some fairly complicated habits, and when he had obtained a stable, perseverative tendency, he brought this into collision with another tendency determined by new stimuli or instruction....

K. Lewin, in our opinion, has been one of the most prominent psychologists to elucidate this question of the artificial production of affect and of experimental disorganization of behaviour. The method of his procedure — the introduction of an emotional setting into the experience of a human, the interest of the subject in the experiment — helped him to obtain an artificial disruption of the affect of considerable strength....

Here the fundamental conception of Lewin is very close to ours. (pp. 206–7)

Who was K. Lewin? He was the very same Kurt Lewin who came to the United States in 1933, founded the Research Center for Group Dynamics at MIT (which later moved to the University of Michigan), and invented "sensitivity training." Shortly before his death in 1947, Lewin founded the National Training Laboratory, which established its campus at Bethel, Maine, under the sponsorship of the National Education Association. There, teachers were instructed in the techniques of sensitivity training and how to become effective change agents.

And so we know from the experiments conducted by Pavlov and Luria in the Soviet Union in the 1920s and '30s, that the psychologists had developed the means artificially to create behavioral disorganization. I submit that the symptoms of dyslexia developed in perfectly normal, physically healthy school children are the result of a collision of reflexes that occurs as the child advances to the second and third grades.

This is how it works. The child is given a sight vocabulary to memorize before he has acquired any phonetic knowledge of our writing system. Subsequently he develops a holistic reflex, that is, the habit of looking at each word as a total configuration and being absorbed at finding something in that configuration to remind the reader of what the word is. (Note: Ach "*formed some fairly complicated habits, and when he had obtained a stable, perseverative tendency, he brought this into collision with another tendency determined by new stimuli or instruction.*")

Many, if not most, children can memorize the shapes of several hundred sight words with significant visual associations. But when the child reaches the second and third grade where the number of words to be learned taxes the memory beyond its capacity, the child experiences a learning breakdown somewhat akin to a nervous breakdown. When the child is then taught some phonics, some letter sounds, ("new stimuli or instruction") as a means of assisting the sight process, the child experiences a conflict or collision of reflexes and develops dyslexia ("disorganisation of behaviour"), the inability to see the phonetic structure of our words, the inability to automatically decode a word. The holistic reflex is simply too strong and the phonetic information too insufficient to overcome the holistic reflex, which then creates a block against seeing our alphabetic words in their phonetic components.

Unless a child is drilled in the letter sounds and can automatically articulate consonant-vowel syllabic combinations, that child will not develop a strong enough phonetic reflex to overcome the holistic reflex and the blockage (cognitive disorganization) it creates. The way, of course, to avoid this problem is to teach the child intensive, systematic phonics first before requiring the child to read whole words.

By teaching this five-year-old child a sight vocabulary before he could master the letter sounds, he was being put on the road to dyslexia. This is particularly harmful because the child's brain at that early age is still in the process of organizing its patterns of thinking, its cerebral habits, habits that are very difficult to unlearn later in life. That accounts for the great difficulty in remediating dyslexics as they grow older and their thinking patterns become more firmly established. It is possible that the brain can be permanently deformed by the early development of thinking patterns based on faulty teaching methods.

Today, millions of American children are being taught to memorize sight words before they even know the alphabet, let alone the letter sounds. Commercial programs sold in supermarkets and bookstores are mostly based on the notion that learning a sight vocabulary is the first step in learning to read. Actually, it's the first step toward becoming a dyslexic. Many parents think they are doing their preschool children a service by purchasing books with audiotapes that permit their children to learn the words in the books by sight while listening to the tapes. They are simply preparing their children to become reading or learning disabled by the time they enter first grade.

Thus, you can see how easy it is to cause dyslexia. Simply have your child memorize a sight vocabulary and develop a holistic reflex. That's all there is to it. That professors of education have perfected the process indicates that they know how it works and what it results in. That is why parents are never warned about teaching their children sight vocabularies. It's a vital part of the dumbing down process that underlies curriculum development in our education system and is supported by professional associations, journals, publishers, federal programs and funding, and the establishment as a whole.

There are exceptions, of course, and they are the individuals inside and outside of the establishment who have been fighting the "system" for years and causing the so-called "reading war." Recent reports inform us that the reading war is over, that the contending parties have reached a compromise: phonics will be taught with whole language. But what is not made clear is how the new pro-phonics policy will be implemented in the schools. The proponents of whole-language have always contended that they do teach phonics. That statement is supposed to satisfy most parents. But what they don't explain is that the kind of incidental phonics they teach does not help the child develop the crucial phonetic reflex.

If the child is simply given phonetic information in the context of a whole language program, that information will not become a reflex. And therefore the child will be reluctant to use that information because it will not be automatic and will require work and will slow down the reading process.

This was proven to me by my own tutoring experience. Some years ago, when a friend of mine enrolled his daughter in public school, I warned him about the possibility that she would become reading disabled because of the teaching methods in today's schools. So he permitted me to start tutoring her in *Alpha-Phonics*. But she was one of these headstrong children who will obey a teacher in school but raise a fuss at being tutored by a family friend. So the tutoring was rather haphazard. In addition, the father had an abiding faith in the public school.

Nevertheless, he was concerned enough to go to the school and insist that his child be taught to read by phonics. So she was put into some sort of "Superkid" class where she was given a little more phonics than in the normal class but not enough to create a phonetic reflex. In that class she was taught to "take risks" and "guess," and her dad thought that this was an excellent technique. He refused to believe that this standard whole-language methodology could create problems. In any case, his daughter wanted to be right and refused to guess, but she was told to guess and that whatever she blurted out would be okay. Meanwhile, the child developed the whole-word habit, proving that you can mess around with a little phonics here and a little phonics there, but it's no substitute for intensive, systematic phonics.

She is now in the third grade and hates to read. Getting her to read is like pulling teeth. Recently I was asked to help her with her reading homework. She is a typical sight reader who makes lots of errors but will not sound out anything because it is too much work. So she makes a fuss when being told to sound out a word. She told me that her teacher said that sounding out is not the best way to read, and since she is still being encouraged to guess at words and skip words, why bother with sounding out at all?

I imagine that there are a lot of parents like my friend who simply assume that the teachers know what they are doing and tend to accept whatever explanations they are given to questions about their children's learning problems. The fact that there are four million children on Ritalin in American schools indicates that parents in general have confidence in their children's educators and are willing to accept whatever they are told by the "experts."

All of which means that only those parents who are concerned enough, informed enough, and willing enough to do what has to be done to save their children from being dumbed down or turned into dyslexics, will know enough to bypass the government schools and provide their children with an education that makes sense. The spectacular growth of the homeschool movement is an indication that more and more parents are doing just that.

THE THEORY OF EVOLUTION: FACT OR FAIRY TALE?

"There are so many flaws in Darwinism that one can wonder why it swept so completely through the scientific world, and why it is still endemic today." — Sir Fred Hoyle

On June 19, 1987, the U.S. Supreme Court struck down a 1981 Louisiana law that mandated a balanced treatment in teaching evolution and creation in public schools. The Court decided that the intent of the law "was clearly to advance the religious viewpoint that a supernatural being created humankind," and therefore violated the First Amendment's prohibition on a government establishment of religion. In other words, the Court adopted the atheist position that creation is a religious myth.

In speaking for the majority, Justice William J. Brennan wrote: "The legislative history documents that the act's primary purpose was to change the science curriculum of public schools in order to provide an advantage to a particular religious doctrine that rejects the factual basis of evolution in its entirety."

We are not surprised that no one saw fit to remind Justice Brennan that some of the world's greatest scientists were and are devout Christians and that atheism is actually destroying true science. But we are surprised that no one on the Louisiana side informed the Justice that there is no "factual basis of evolution." It is all theory and speculation, and each year the theory becomes less and less tenable in the light of new scientific evidence.

Nevertheless, many state departments of education have taken the Court's decision to be a green light for the aggressive teaching of evolution as fact and the exclusion of any reference to creationism in public school biology courses.

In the light of this hostile anti-creationist trend, it is important for us to do what the Court failed to do: review the theory of evolu-

43

tion and determine what indeed are the "facts."

First, what exactly is the theory of evolution? For the answer, we must go to the source: Charles Darwin's famous book, *On the Origin of Species*, published in 1859. Darwin claims that the thousands of different species of animals, insects, and plants that exist on earth were not the works of a Divine Creator who made each species in its present immutable form, as described in Genesis, but are the products of a very long natural process of development from simpler organic forms to more complex organic forms.

Thus, according to Darwin, species continue to change, or "evolve," through a process of natural selection in which nature's harsh conditions permit only the fittest to survive in more adaptable forms.

These views, of course, had considerable moral and religious implications. Ronald Clark, in his biography of Darwin, wrote:

> There were two separate parts to the theory that, while offensive to the religious establishment in themselves, acquired their real danger — like the two halves of a nuclear weapon — when they were brought together. One was that species had not been created by God but had evolved over the years; the other was that evolution had not been directed by God but had been governed by the apparently fortuitous facts of natural selection. While Darwin was proud of his theory of natural selection, his most important single contribution to the evolutionary argument, he saw as one of its main virtues the fact that it provided a counterblow to the idea of creation.

Darwin also believed that all life originated from a single source — a kind of primeval slime in which the first living organisms formed spontaneously out of nonliving matter through a random process. These organisms are supposed to have branched off into different forms — plants, insects, and animals.

Evolutionists have worked out all sorts of fascinating genealogical diagrams purporting to show the descent and relationship of one species to another. But what they don't tell the public is that all of the connections in these family trees are based on pure speculation and conjecture. Sir Fred Hoyle wrote:

It has been through the device of presenting such diagrams with the presumed connections drawn in firm solid lines that the general scientific world has been bamboozled into believing that evolution has been proved. Nothing could be further from the truth.... The absence from the fossil record of the intermediate forms required by the usual evolutionary theory shows that *if* terrestrial life-forms have evolved from a common stock, the major branchings in the evolutionary tree must have developed very quickly. And the major branchings, *if* they occurred, were accompanied by genetic changes that were not small. (p. 87)

Probably the most controversial aspect of Darwin's theory was that concerning man's place in the evolutionary scheme. In his book, *The Descent of Man*, published in 1870, Darwin contended that man and ape were evolutionary cousins with a common ancestor. When it came to the mind, to intelligence, the gap between man and the other animals, Darwin believed, was one of degree.

In his notebook he had written: "Man in his arrogance thinks himself a great work worthy the interposition of a deity. [M]ore humble & I think truer to consider him created from animals."

But the fossil record revealing the different stages of man's evolution from apelike creature to Homo sapiens has not been found. Paleoanthropologists have hunted high and low for the missing link or links. But not only have they not found them, they are now pretty sure that such links do not exist. So instead of admitting defeat, they've proclaimed victory! According to David Pilbeam, a paleoanthropologist at Harvard: "We should no longer say that we are descended from apes. We *are* apes" (*Discover*, July 1983, p. 23).

In other words, since there is no missing link, one must conclude that men and apes are actually one and the same species! If that is the case, then why call men apes? Why not call apes men? Of course, if we did that, we would not be able to experiment on apes in the laboratory. We would have to extend to them our notion of human rights, which, incidentally, we do not extend to preborn human beings.

All of which means that some scientists are willing to accept a bigger lie if the smaller lie cannot be proven true. Apparently, to some scientists, any lie is preferable to accepting the possibility that a Creator had something to do with everything that exists.

The simple fact is that no proof whatsoever has been found indicating that one species evolves into another. The fossil record is simply a series of still pictures of species that existed at one time. They do not show how one species evolves into another. Transitional fossils have not been found. The fossil record shows new species appearing suddenly without any ancestors. What scientific investigation indicates is that the species are immutable and that when mutations occur, they do not become new species. For example, evolutionists have been experimenting with fruit flies for years in the hope of demonstrating evolution at work. But the fruit flies have stubbornly refused to develop into anything but more fruit flies, despite all kinds of stimuli, including radiation. Some mutations have occurred, but nothing to suggest the beginnings of a new species.

In other words, lions have remained lions, monkeys have remained monkeys, and cats have remained cats. Different breeds and varieties may exist within a species, but nature places built-in genetic obstacles to evolutionary change. And when you consider that our museums are now filled with over 100 million fossils of 250,000 different species and not a single series of transitional forms has been found among them, one begins to suspect that a gigantic hoax is being perpetrated by the scientists. In fact, gaps between major groups of organisms have been growing even wider and more undeniable. And so it is hard to understand how scientists can assert that evolution is fact and still call themselves scientists. Even Dr. Stephen Jay Gould, a passionate defender of evolution, has written: "The fossil record with its abrupt transitions offers no support for gradual change" (*Natural History*, June–July 1977, pp. 22–30).

Even Darwin wrote in *On the Origin of Species*:

> [T]he geological record is extremely imperfect … and [this fact] will to a large extent explain why we do not find interminable varieties, connecting together all the extinct and existing forms of life by the finest graduated steps. He who rejects these views on the nature of the geological record, will rightly reject my whole theory. (pp. 341–42)

Apparently, even after 130 years of intensive but frustrating research, today's proponents of evolution are unwilling to take Darwin's own advice.

As for the origin of life, there is no fossil evidence whatsoever to support the supposition that all life came from a common ancestor. In fact, not only the fossil evidence but the genetic evidence as well points toward creation as the source of life. The evidence for creation is now so palpable that some scientists, convinced that life could not have originated as Darwin believed, are now theorizing that life, in a variety of forms, was sent to earth from outer space by some form of intelligence.

As for the theory that life originated by accident in some sort of chemical soup, it was Louis Pasteur who proved that spontaneous generation is impossible. He contended that every generation of every living creature had to be derived from a preceding generation. Life could not have started spontaneously from inorganic matter.

But evolutionists have kept on hoping that they could produce life from nonlife. In the 1950s Stanley Miller performed a famous experiment that synthesized amino acids from hypothetical components of the earth's original atmosphere. The experiment did not produce life from nonlife, for the distance from amino acid to life is immense.

In other words, the spontaneous-generation-of-life idea is just wishful thinking on the part of evolutionists. Dr. Fred Hoyle has calculated that such an accident had one chance in ten to the power of 40,000 of occurring, making it beyond possibility. Now that we know of the enormous complexity of the DNA genetic code and that the information content of a simple cell has been estimated as around ten to the power of twelve bits, we know that random development of living matter is an impossibility. Consider these facts: there are 2,000 complex enzymes required for a living organism, but not a single one of them could have formed accidentally. The genes of the simplest single-celled organism contain more data than there are letters in all of the volumes of the world's largest library. As Dr. Fred Hoyle has put it:

> The chance that higher life forms might have emerged in this [accidental] way is comparable with the chance that a tornado

sweeping through a junk-yard might assemble a Boeing 747 from the materials therein. (*Nature*, 11/12/81, p. 105)

Yet one evolutionist has gone so far as to say that given enough time, monkeys typing on typewriters could eventually type out the complete works of Shakespeare. To this Luther Sunderland has replied:

> If there were monkeys typing on typewriters covering every square foot of the Earth's surface and each one typed at random at the fantastic rate of ten characters a second for thirty billion years, there wouldn't be the slightest reasonable chance that a single one would type out a single specific five-word sentence of thirty-one letters, spaces and punctuation. The actual probability is less than one chance in a trillion. (p. 61)

To sum it all up: the fossil record does not support the idea of gradual evolution; it supports creation. Orthodox evolutionists call it punctuated equilibrium; Hoyle calls it cosmic creationism. Nor does the fossil record support the idea of a common accidental source of all life. Evidences of common ancestry have not been found. In addition, Louis Pasteur debunked the idea of the spontaneous generation of living organic matter from nonliving, inanimate matter.

Does inanimate matter, left to the vagaries of chance and accident, have the inherent ability over a long period of time to develop spontaneously into more complex, higher levels of organization? The Second Law of Thermodynamics says no. This law indicates "that nature tends to go from order to disorder; from complexity to simplicity. If the most random arrangement of energy is uniform distribution, then the present arrangement of the energy in the universe is nonrandom" (Thaxton, *The Mystery of Life's Origin*, p. 115).

In other words, the present arrangement of energy in the universe must be the result of a creative force, for matter by itself cannot and does not behave creatively.

The evolutionists have not been able to explain how inanimate matter, with its inherent tendency to decay, reversed itself so as to be able to synthesize life and to build complex organisms. That would have required matter, on its own, to develop the highly complex genetic codes found in the DNA molecule.

If all that we have said thus far is true, then why is evolution taught as fact and creationism kept out of the schools? Because all of modern secular education is based on the assumption that evolution is fact.

Progressive, or humanist, education is evolutionary theory put into practice in the classroom. Progressive education grew out of the new experimental psychology based on the belief that man is an animal, a product of evolution with common ancestry with the ape, and could therefore be studied like any other animal. In Germany, where the new psychology originated, Darwin's main support came from Ernst Haeckel, who maintained that psychology was a branch of physiology and that mind could therefore be fitted into the scheme of evolution. Haeckel was also responsible for the idea that during embryological development higher organisms like man relived their evolutionary history—that ontogeny recapitulates phylogeny.

That hypothesis has since been proven false, but it has become the basis of the way reading is taught in most American schools. The look-say method of teaching reading was promoted by the progressives on the ground that children should go through the different stages that the human race went through in learning to read: pictography, ideographs, and finally the alphabet. The application of the dictum that "ontogeny recapitulates phylogeny" in reading instruction has led to a literacy disaster.

All of educational psychology today is based on evolutionary thinking. The stimulus-response techniques of teaching developed by Edward L. Thorndike, John B. Watson, Ivan Pavlov, and B. F. Skinner are all derived from Darwin. John B. Watson, in *Behaviorism* wrote:

> Darwin and also Lange emphasized the stimulus arousing the emotional response and the reaction to it. Their objective descriptions of fear reactions are classical and thoroughly objective and behavioristic. (p. 141)

Thorndike, the father of behaviorist educational psychology, wrote in 1911 in his book *Animal Intelligence*:

Nowhere more truly than in his mental capacities is man a part of nature. His instincts, that is, his inborn tendencies to feel and act in certain ways, show throughout marks of kinship with the lower animals, especially with our nearest relatives physically, the monkeys. His sense-powers show no new creation. His intellect we have seen to be a simple though extended variation from the general animal sort. This again is presaged by the similar variation in the case of the monkeys. Amongst the minds of animals that of man leads, not as a demigod from another planet, but as a king from the same race. (p. 294)

Thorndike summed up progressive teaching techniques in the following unforgettable sentence:

The best way with children may often be, in the pompous words of an animal trainer, "to arrange everything in connection with the trick so that the animal will be compelled by the laws of his own nature to perform it." (Ibid., pp. 104–5)

In addition, the moral philosophy of the progressives is humanism, which is now the general moral philosophy of public education. The first tenets of humanism, as explained in the Humanist Manifesto, published in 1933, are:

Tenet 1: Religious humanists regard the universe as self-existing and not created.
Tenet 2: Humanism believes that man is a part of nature and that he has emerged as the result of a continuous process.

Thus, both the psychology and philosophy of public education are based on the false doctrines of Darwinian evolution.

Dr. Fred Hoyle wrote: "There are so many flaws in Darwinism that one can wonder why it swept so completely through the scientific world, and why it is still endemic today."

Of course, we know the reason why. The entire liberal-humanist scientific establishment espouses a worldview that emphatically denies the existence of God. Modern morality is based on the notion that man is an animal, there is no sin, and that sexual repression is unhealthy and causes neuroses.

But liberated modern morality has not produced mental health but social anarchy, rampant venereal disease, mental breakdowns, suicide, drug addiction, increased crime, etc. Valium is now the largest selling drug in America. Modern morality has produced unprecedented stress, depression, and emotional confusion, and the only answer the humanists have for all of this human misery is drugs.

Since both the theory and practice of contemporary public education are for the most part based on the theories and teachings of the progressives, all of whom believed that the theory of evolution applied to the development of mind as well as physical attributes, one can say without fear of contradiction that the public school is a perfect reflection of the evolutionary humanist worldview. As French biologist Jacques Monad put it:

> Man has to understand that he is a mere accident. Not only is man not the center of creation; he is not even the heir to a sort of predetermined evolution that would have produced either man or something very like him in any case. (Judson, *The Eighth Day of Creation*, p. 217)

Note, incidentally, how similar Monad's view of man is to Darwin's that man should be brought down to the animal level where he belongs.

In other words, what the public school tells the child is that there is no God, no Creator; that life originated by accident; and that there is no meaning or purpose to life other than the satisfaction of animal needs and desires. And what the behavioral psychologists tell the teachers is that children can be taught like animals by techniques developed in laboratories in which animals were the subjects of experimentation.

This is particularly true in the teaching of reading in the primary schools by way of the look-say method. In 1940, Professor Walter Dearborn, head of educational psychology at Harvard, described the methodology as follows:

> The principle which we have used to explain the acquisition of a sight vocabulary is, of course, the one suggested by Pavlov's well known experiments on the conditioned response. This is

> as it should be. The basic process involved in conditioning and
> in learning to read is the same. (*School and Society*, 10/19/40,
> p. 368)

Thus, animal training techniques have become the basis of reading
instruction in American schools. The result, of course, has been massive reading failure, for the simple reason that children are not animals and cannot be taught as animals. Animals can be trained but
not educated. Children can both be trained and educated, and when
it comes to reading, it is better to educate than to train.

The application of behavioral psychology to teaching has literally destroyed academic standards to the point where we are now
considered a nation at risk. To expect our students to achieve academic excellence while excluding the development of the intellect,
which the behaviorists are doing, is like Pharaoh demanding that the
Israelites make bricks without straw.

Fortunately, many of our young people are resilient and healthy
enough to survive the public school's harm. But millions of others are
not so fortunate and have become the functional illiterates and intellectual cripples that plague our society.

Despite its falsehood, the theory of evolution has been integrated into our popular culture as truth. For example, this is what
the 1977 edition of the *Standard Family Reference Encyclopedia* says
about evolution:

> Life probably first evolved from the primeval soup some 3000–
> 4000 million years ago when the first organic chemicals were
> synthesized due to the effects of lightning. Primitive algae ca-
> pable of synthesizing their own food material have been found
> in geological formations some 2000 million years old. Simple
> forms of animals and fungi then evolved. From that time there
> has been a slow evolution of multicellular organisms.

Someday the average educated American will be able to read that
paragraph and understand it for what it is: a fairy tale. In the first
place, spontaneous generation is impossible even with such primitive
forms as viruses. Second, because of the enormous complexity of living matter, the random, accidental self-creation of life is mathemati-

cally impossible. Third, why would living matter randomly develop the need or desire to eat or continue living? Why would it *want* to continue living? Would the algae's quality of life in the primeval soup be so wonderful that it would develop this remarkable urge to keep living? As for "slow evolution," not even the evolutionists believe in that anymore. They now believe in "punctuated equilibrium" in order to explain the sudden appearance of species without ancestors. And fourth, matter tends to go from order to disorder, which implies the existence of a creative force that could reverse that tendency.

So much for Darwin's theory of evolution. But some of the most intelligent people in America take it to be fact. For example, former Secretary of Education William Bennett once told John Lofton in an interview: "I believe there is good scientific evidence for evolution."

It's apparent that Mr. Bennett did not know his facts. But even more shocking is the statement made by George F. Will in a column (*Idaho Statesman*, 6/26/87):

> Facts are revisable data about the world. Theories are supposed to interpret facts. Evolution is a fact about which there are various explanatory theories.

If evolution is a "fact," someone has yet to prove it! The problem with Mr. Will is that he is probably confusing evolution with breeding. Breeding, and the existence of a variety of breeds within a species, is a function of genetics, not evolution.

Meanwhile, our schools will turn out more generations of Americans believing that evolution is fact and the Bible a fairy tale.

References

Clark, Ronald W., *The Survival of Charles Darwin*, Random House, New York, NY; 1984.

Darwin, Charles, *On the Origin of Species*, A Facsimile of the First Edition, Harvard University Press, Cambridge, MA; 1964.

Hoyle, Sir Fred and Wickramasinghe, Chandra, *Evolution from Space*, Simon & Schuster, New York, NY; 1981.

Jusdon, Horace F., *The Eighth Day of Creation*, Simon & Schuster, New York, NY; 1979.

Kautz, Darrel, *The Origin of Living Things*, 10025 West Nash St., Milwaukee, WI 53222; 1988.

Sunderland, Luther D., *Darwin's Enigma*, Master Book Publishers, P.O. Box 606, El Cajon, CA 92022; 1984.

Thaxton, Charles B., Bradley, Walter L., and Olsen, Roger L., *The Mystery of Life's Origin*, Philosophical Library, New York, NY; 1984.

HOW PROGRESSIVE EDUCATORS PLANNED TO SOCIALIZE AMERICA

Most Americans who have become aware of the academic and moral decline of public education, tend to believe that the humanistic curriculum that now dominates the system is of relatively recent origin. They believe that the great emphasis now placed on the "affective domain"—all of those programs devoted to values, feelings, activities, behavior, group dynamics, sexuality, etc.— is somewhat new. Actually, it is far from new. The fact is that the groundwork for what we have in our schools today was laid early in this century by the Progressives who knew exactly where they wanted to lead America: to a socialist society.

The Progressives were a new breed of educator that came on the scene in the late nineteenth century. These men, members of the Protestant academic elite, no longer believed in the religion of their fathers. They put their new faith in science, evolution, and psychology. Science provided the means to know the material world. Evolution explained the origin of man, relegating the story of Genesis to mythology. And psychology institutionalized the scientific study of human nature and provided the future, scientific means to control human behavior.

Many of these Progressives studied in Germany under Professor Wilhelm Wundt, the father of experimental psychology. Among the most noteworthy were G. Stanley Hall, James McKeen Cattell, Charles Judd, James Earl Russell, James R. Angell, and Frank E. Spaulding. They brought back to America Wundt's teachings and methodology and set up psychology labs of their own in American universities. In these labs man was to be studied scientifically as one would study an animal. But since human beings could not be experimented on in labs, the psychologists used animals.

In 1928, Professor Edward L. Thorndike, head of educational psychology at Teachers College, Columbia University, wrote:

> [E]xperiments on learning in the lower animals have probably
> contributed more to knowledge of education, per hour or per
> unit of intellect spent, than experiments on children.

He also wrote:

> The best way with children may often be, in the pompous
> words of an animal trainer, "to arrange everything in connec-
> tion with the trick so that the animal will be compelled by the
> laws of his own nature to perform it."

Out of this methodology emerged behavioral psychology. In distinguishing behaviorism from earlier introspective psychologies, John
B. Watson wrote that the behavioral psychologist "must describe the
behavior of man in no other terms than those you would use in describing the behavior of the ox you slaughter."

The behavioral psychologist studies only what can be seen and
measured in human behavior. Watson wrote:

> Behaviorism claims that consciousness is neither a definite nor
> a usable concept. The behaviorist ... holds, further, that belief
> in the existence of consciousness goes back to the ancient days
> of superstition and magic.

The progressive-behaviorist curriculum thus consists mainly of animal training. For example, in the field of reading instruction, Professor Walter Dearborn of Harvard described the look-say method of
teaching reading as follows (*School and Society*, 10/19/40):

> The Principle which we have used to explain the acquisition of
> a sight vocabulary is, of course, the one suggested by Pavlov's
> well-known experiments on the conditioned response. This is
> as it should be. The basic process involved in conditioning and
> in learning to read is the same.

That the ultimate goal of behaviorism is the control of human behavior was spelled out quite plainly by John B. Watson in his book,
Behaviorism (p. 11):

> The interest of the behaviorist in man's doings is more than the interest of the spectator — he wants to control man's reactions as physical scientists want to control and manipulate other natural phenomena. It is the business of behavioristic psychology to be able to predict and to control human activity.

The Progressives' plan to socialize America required the most thorough and radical reform of American education. To this they applied their extensive knowledge of behavioral psychology. That the goal was socialism was clearly known and understood throughout the educational establishment. That it meant downgrading academics in favor of socialization was also understood, for in a socialist society an elite rules at the top, and the masses below are relegated to the subservient, mindless tasks of an industrial system.

Professor Dallas Johnson of the University of Washington wrote in 1915 in an article entitled "Socializing Education":

> Scholastic traditions and academic prejudices must give way to the ideal of increasing the social solidarity of our people. (*School and Society*, 12/18/15)

Dr. Charles W. Eliot, President of Harvard, in 1916 advocated reform that would hasten the shift from academics to vocational activities. He wrote:

> The changes which ought to be made immediately in the programmes of American secondary schools, in order to correct the glaring deficiencies of the present programmes are chiefly: introduction of more hand, ear and eye-work — such as drawing, carpentry, tuning, music, sewing and cooking. (School and Society, 3/18/16)

Professor Walter R. Smith, of State Normal School, Emporia, Kansas, in an article entitled "The Fundamentals of a Socialized Educational Program," wrote in 1918:

> The process of socialization will require greater emphasis upon the social studies in our schools. The linguistic and mathematical core of the old classical curriculum must give way to a social core. (*School and Society*, 7/13/18)

All of these men reflected the thinking of John Dewey, who had written in 1898:

> There is … a false educational god whose idolators are legion, and whose cult influences the entire educational system. This is language-study — the study not of foreign language, but of English; not in higher, but in primary education.

> The plea for the predominance of learning to read in early school-life because of the great importance attaching to literature seems to me a perversion.

Why did these men believe in socialism? Because, as atheists, they were convinced that socialism offered the only salvation from evil. To them the causes of evil were societal: ignorance, poverty, and social injustice. As evolutionists they rejected such concepts as sin, innate depravity, or the fall of man. They thus attributed the causes of social injustice to capitalism, individualism, and religion. By substituting socialism, collectivism and atheism in their place, they had no doubt that heaven on earth was quite attainable.

The Progressives knew that the new society they were trying to build required of them extraordinary efforts and devotion. Their vision included a globalist humanism, which was well expressed in a speech given in 1918 by Professor Charles H. Judd, the Wundtian dean of the School of Education at the University of Chicago. Judd said:

> I am arguing for a new kind of humanism…. We must build in the future a social structure for which there is no pattern. The humanism of the future will be dependent, not on imitation, but on self-determination….

> I have been reading, as I am sure many of you have, the platform of the English labor party. Its program of social reform and of education for more intelligent citizenship makes a profound appeal to every lover of democracy. I believe the English labor party is right….

> The social psychology of the future will recognize different mental patterns no less than does the psychology of today, but

it will exhibit a new factor, namely, conscious devotion to social solidarity....

Perhaps the time will come when the psychological differences of nations will be assimilated into a larger pattern of intelligent appreciation of the solidarity of a rational humanity. (*School and Society*, 9/10/18)

Some educators indulged in messianic hyperbole when writing of this globalist vision. One such educator was Professor J. E. Boodin of Carleton College who wrote in 1918 while World War I was still raging:

If the German junkers have been willing and eager to undergo a life of discipline and sacrifice to promote the illusion of Pangermany, how much more should we be willing to bear and do for Panhumanity, for an ideal humanity — counting its riches to promote the general well being, finding our soul in sacrificial cooperation with our fellows, realizing that the only thing that is eternal and worth striving for is the good life. Thus shall we make the pattern laid up in heaven incarnate on earth. Thus shall we build the city of God.

Indeed, such "sacrificial cooperation" was needed to carry out the full program of educational reform that would create the new humanist utopia. The organizational mastermind who engineered this reform was Charles H. Judd who, in 1915, organized the Cleveland Conference, a semi-secret annual meeting of top educators. Judd urged the members of the conference to undertake "the positive and aggressive task of ... a detailed reorganization of the materials of instruction in schools of all grades."

It was Judd's protégé, William Scott Gray, who created the Dick and Jane look-say reading instruction program that was to start America on its literacy decline. In 1955, when *Why Johnny Can't Read* was published, Gray organized the International Reading Association to insure that look-say would dominate reading instruction in American primary schools for decades to come despite the mounting opposition of parents.

By 1920 the reform movement had progressed so far that Professor M. V. O'Shea of the University of Wisconsin, reporting on the Cleveland Conference of 1920, wrote:

> The schools are moving with an irresistible force on to a program based on the doctrine that pupils must have work in the schools which will interpret the world outside for them and help them to adjust themselves thereto.
>
> ... There were no terms used by the speakers, except by two or three adherents to the ancient order, which indicated the slightest belief in the doctrine that the schools should adopt a curriculum and methods of teaching designed merely to exercise the minds of pupils; the doctrine of formal discipline is passed. (*School and Society*, 3/27/20)

The Progressives also realized that if their plan was to succeed, they would need the cooperation of America's teachers. In 1917 they took control of the National Education Association and established its permanent headquarters in Washington, D.C., where they hoped to exert maximum influence on the federal government. Professor George Strayer of Teachers College, Columbia, and president of the NEA in 1919 told that year's convention:

> When our half million teachers agree upon educational policies and make insistent demands in keeping with national progress, these demands will be heard in Congress. (*School and Society*, 7/19/19)

In 1924 Professor Edwin D. Starbuck of the University of Iowa told an NEA convention:

> We are now gaining conscious control of human development. The future of humanity, the destiny of nations, the direction of human progress, are in the hands not so much of makers of laws or captains of industry as of teachers who are shaping the citizenry of the world.

The 1920s and '30s were devoted to a total transformation of the public school curriculum. Charles Judd told a meeting of the American Political Science Association in 1931 that the entire organized profession was now engaged in the process of promoting "a movement to bring to full realization the project of socializing the whole body of instructional material in schools and colleges."

The work, in fact, was being done so vigorously that a reporter, attending the 1932 meeting of the NEA's school superintendents' department, held in Washington, D.C., and attended by John Dewey, Charles Judd and other Progressives, wrote:

> Here, in the very citadel of capitalism ... this group of outstanding spokesmen of American education talked a remarkably strong brand of socialism.

And you can be sure that if a superintendent wanted to advance his career, he had to tow the socialist line.

Some of these "outstanding spokesmen of American education" had toured Soviet Russia in 1928 and come back with glowing reports about the communist experiment.

Even the American Historical Association got into the act of preparing America for socialism. In 1934 its Commission on the Social Studies reported:

> The report makes it clear that two social philosophies are now struggling for supremacy: individualism, with its attending capitalism and classicism, and collectivism, with planned economy and mass rights. Believing that present trends indicate the victory of the latter, the Commission on the Social Studies offers a comprehensive blueprint by which education may prepare to meet the demands of a collectivist social order without submerging the individual as a helpless victim of bureaucratic control.

And so the new purpose of public education was *to prepare America for socialism.*

Is it any wonder that so many of us emerged from public schools totally ignorant of the true nature of the free-enterprise system? Is it any wonder that the first thing Americans now cry for when something goes wrong is government regulation or control?

Is it any wonder that the farmers of America have ceased to believe in the marketplace and look to the government for their sustenance? We have been so brainwashed to believe in paternal government that most Americans cannot even conceive of education without government ownership or control.

The Progressives did their job exceedingly well, and their disciples today, in the highest positions of power in the educational establishment, still press that globalist vision while centralizing all education under state monopoly control. Their political power is enormous, thanks to the NEA, which is convincing more and more legislators to pour more and more tax money down the educational rathole.

Meanwhile, public education has become a moral and academic disaster. But Americans have grown to live with it. They know something is wrong, but they have no idea what to do about it.

Fortunately, there is a growing number of parents who know what is going on and have removed their children from the government schools. This trend will continue to grow despite the determination of the "educators" to crush it.

As we have shown, what we have today is the result of a very long process. Indeed, the process was expected to be long, for as John Dewey wrote in 1898:

> Change must come gradually. To force it unduly would compromise its final success by favoring a violent reaction.

Americans are now in a position to see quite clearly where the educators want to take us. The goal is a world socialist government in which individual freedom and national independence will be lost forever. Clearly this is not what the American people want. And so, the conflict between the educators and the people will persist indefinitely.

ENEMIES IN ACADEME

The secularization of the American university began with the takeover of Harvard by the Unitarians in 1805. Harvard had been founded in 1636 by Puritan Calvinists who recognized the necessity for training up a learned clergy if the new Bible commonwealth was to flourish in the wilderness. Since 1620, some 17,000 Puritans had migrated to New England, and they wanted ministers who were able to expound the Scriptures from the original Hebrew and Greek, as well as be familiar with what the church fathers, scholastic philosophers, and reformists had written in Greek and Latin.

The kind of teaching that Harvard was to provide was spelled out in its *Rules and Precepts* as follows:

> Let every Student be plainly instructed, and earnestly pressed to consider well, the maine end of his life and studies is, to know God and Jesus Christ which is eternal life, John 17:3, and therefore to lay Christ in the bottome, as the only foundation of all knowledge and learning....

Actually, the Unitarian takeover in 1805 was preceded by a protracted struggle between orthodoxy and liberalism that began in 1701 when Increase Mather stepped down from the presidency. In 1707, the liberals, who had obtained a definite majority in the governing Corporation, elected John Leverett as president of Harvard. Leverett, a religious liberal and a layman, set the college on its course away from Calvinist orthodoxy.

Under Leverett, Harvard became known as a place where young men became gentlemen rather than scholars. Leverett differed from his predecessors, who regarded Harvard merely as a seminary for orthodox Congregational ministers. According to Samuel Eliot Morison's *Three Centuries of Harvard*:

> Former presidents like to refer to Harvard men in commencement orations and the like by the Old Testament phrase *filli*

prophetarum, "Sons of the Prophets." Leverett called the alumni Harvardinates, or "Sons of Harvard."

It was also under Leverett that Harvard began attracting the unfavorable attention of the press, which reported on students living "in riot and luxury." Leverett's own diary reveals that the faculty was having plenty of trouble with "profane swearing," "riotous Actions," and "bringing Cards into the College." An undergraduate's diary of the time notes that the students were frequently slipping off to Boston for horse races, pirate hangings, and other diversions. Liberalism was already producing its inevitable by-products.

In 1720, Thomas Hollis, a London merchant, endowed the Hollis Professorship of Divinity, Harvard's first professorial chair. In 1721, Edward Wigglesworth, a talented young cleric, was appointed to it. Although Wigglesworth satisfied the orthodox members of the Corporation as to his adherence to Calvinist doctrine, he soon showed his true colors.

Morison wrote:

> One of the first theologians in New England who dared publicly to challenge the "five points of Calvinism," he employed the deadly method of doubt and inquiry, rather than direct attack.... Wigglesworth was a prime favorite with Harvard students, and he and his son Edward, who succeeded him, had a very great influence on New England theology. It was the Wigglesworths who trained the pioneers of liberal Christianity in New England — the ministers who lead the way out of the lush but fearsome jungle of Calvinism, into the thin, clear light of Unitarianism.

The founding of Yale College in 1701 at New Haven, Connecticut, by orthodox Harvard graduates was a reaction to the growing liberalism at Harvard. Yale, in fact, was to carry on the orthodox tradition well into the nineteenth century before it too succumbed to liberalism.

That the religious liberalism of the Harvard elite did not reflect the true feelings of the average man in the colonies became quite obvious during the Great Awakening, which began in the 1730s. In September 1740, George Whitefield, the fiery evangelical revivalist, arrived in Boston and addressed 15,000 people on Boston Common. He was invited to Harvard, where the students were eager and attentive but the faculty was rather cool. On a subsequent visit to the Boston area, Whitefield was not even invited to Harvard. Henceforth, he and his followers began to denounce Harvard as a house of impiety and sin. As a result, Harvard began to suffer a decline in enrollment. Yale, on the other hand, now required that "the students should be established in the principles of religion according to the [Westminster] Assembly's Catechism." Also, every officer of the college was required to subscribe publicly to the Westminster Confession of Faith and the Saybrook Platform of the Congregational churches of Connecticut before assuming his duties.

Morison wrote:

> On the whole, Harvard succeeded in keeping far ahead of popular religious prejudice, and so far independent of sectarian control, as the times and circumstances made wise and possible. Too abrupt a change in religious matters would have isolated Harvard in the New England community, diminished her usefulness, and, at the time of the Revolution, endangered her existence. There are still those who believe that, by keeping the Calvinist machine running, Yale and Princeton conserved certain values that were dissipated at Cambridge in the exhaust of Unitarianism; but it is difficult nowadays to imagine a Harvard linked up with fundamentalism.

Although the Great Awakening had little effect on the Harvard elite, it gave tremendous impetus to God-centered education elsewhere in the colonies. In 1746, the Philadelphia Presbyterian Synod secured a charter for the College of New Jersey, which in 1756 became Princeton College. Most of its first six presidents, Jonathan Edwards among them, had been prominent preachers in the revival movement.

In 1766, members of the Dutch Reformed Church founded Queen's College, which sixty years later became Rutgers at New Brunswick, New Jersey. In 1764, Baptists founded Brown University in Providence, Rhode Island, and in 1769 a Congregational preacher by the name of Eleazar Wheelock founded Dartmouth College in New Hampshire. Even the non-sectarian University of Pennsylvania, founded in 1756 with the help of Benjamin Franklin, welcomed preachers to edify the students. In short, the religious fervor, which also kindled the flame of freedom that brought on the struggle for independence, greatly diminished the influence of Harvard until well after the Revolutionary War had ended.

The rise of Unitarianism among the academic and merchant elite in Puritan New England might seem at first a highly unlikely occurrence. But universities, as we so well know, seem to attract men of intellectual pride who gaze longingly on the tree of knowledge of good and evil, thinking that if they eat of its fruit, they will be as gods.

In 1785, under the ministry of Harvard-educated Unitarian James Freeman, the congregation of King's Chapel in Boston removed from their Anglican liturgy all references to the Trinity, thus establishing the first Unitarian church in America. Twenty years later, the Unitarian takeover of Harvard was complete.

The rebellion against Calvinism was a rebellion against the Biblical view of man and God. William Ellery Channing, a Harvard alumnus who became leader of the Unitarian movement, explained the basis of Unitarianism at the dedication of a new Unitarian church in Baltimore in 1817. After dismissing the concept of the Trinity as "an enormous tax on credulity," he then zeroed in on God Himself:

> We believe in the moral perfection of God.... It is not because he is our Creator merely, but because he created us for good and holy purposes: it is not because his will is irresistible, but because his will is the perfection of virtue, that we pay him allegiance. We cannot bow before a being, however great and powerful, who governs tyrannically. We respect nothing but excellence whether on earth or in heaven. We venerate, not the loftiness of God's throne, but the equity and goodness in which it is established....
>
> Now we object to the systems of religion which prevail among us, that they are adverse, in a greater or less degree, to these purifying, comforting, and honorable views of God, that they take from us our father in heaven, and substitute for him a being, whom we cannot love if we would, and whom we ought not to love if we could.

For Unitarians, the worship of God depended on His being what they thought He should be, not what He actually was. In any case, Jesus was reduced to the status of prophet and teacher. He was divine only to the extent that we are all divine. Salvation was no longer attained exclusively through Christ but through a good education and good works.

The Unitarians also rejected the Calvinist view of man as being innately depraved. Man, they were convinced, was not only basically good, but morally perfectible. For this reason, social action became the principle mode in which Unitarians practiced their religion. They were convinced that evil was caused not by man's sinful nature, but by ignorance, poverty, and social injustice.

By eliminating ignorance through universal public education, they would eliminate poverty, which in turn would eliminate social injustice. Once this was done and the happy results observed by all, the Unitarians would have proven that they were philosophically and theologically right and that the Calvinists were wrong.

This necessity to prove the rightness of their beliefs became the driving force behind the Unitarians' political and social activism. It provided the messianic impetus to promote universal public education, and it fired the excesses of the abolitionist movement that eventually led to the Civil War.

While the early Harvard Unitarians believed that their rational form of Christianity was quite scriptural, the newer generation, influenced by the Enlightenment and the intoxicating elixir of Hegelian pantheism, saw no reason why they should subject their emotional, spiritual, and intellectual aspirations to the stultifying restrictions of the Bible.

Thus it was that in 1838, Ralph Waldo Emerson shocked the older Unitarians with his famous Divinity School Address, in which he offered a devastating critique of all organized religion. Through the new movement of transcendentalism, Emerson was able to release Unitarians from the weak bonds that still connected them to the religion of the Bible. Transcendentalism was the new form of spirituality that elevated man to godhood. It was far more compatible with the Eastern religions than with the religion of the ancient Hebrews.

Meanwhile, Harvard became the Unitarian Vatican, a self-governing principality on the banks of the Charles River, a citadel of humanist liberalism. When America's oldest, richest, and most prestigious university becomes the nation's foremost antagonist of orthodox Biblical religion, it is bound to have a spiritually devastating influence on American cultural and intellectual life.

E. J. Kahn wrote in *Harvard, Through Change and Through Storm*:

> Other appraisers of Harvard have compared it to a tiny part of Europe — specifically, to the Vatican. Members of the Corporation, among whose responsibilities is the selection of Harvard's president, have compared themselves to the College of Cardinals.

> No president of Harvard is known to have invested himself publicly with Papal stature, but the analogy has its points. Harvard has traditionally operated like a small, powerful, and subjectively infallible political entity with a worldwide constituency....

> It is one of Harvard's special problems that it has long been conscious of being a superpower — king, as it were, of the academic mountain.

The road to secularization among other great private American universities was somewhat similar. Yale, Princeton, William and Mary, Brown, Dartmouth, and Columbia were founded by Anglicans, Presbyterians, and Congregationalists. However, as the Protestant sects became liberal, the universities followed suit.

At Yale, the departure from orthodoxy was spurred by the profound influence of German Hegelian philosophy. Georg Friedrich Hegel (1770–1831) was probably the most influential philosopher of his time — and probably the most influential of ours if we consider his influence on the Marxists who permeate American universities.

Hegel rejected the theology of the Bible and believed that everything in the universe is "God." In this pantheistic universe, "God" is in the process of perfecting himself through a dynamic evolutionary process known as the dialectic — a constant, endless struggle between the thesis and the antithesis, which then resolve themselves into a synthesis. This synthesis then becomes the new thesis, which then inevitably forms a new antithesis to continue the progressive struggle onward and upward toward perfection. It was this dialectic concept of progress that became the basis of the "progressive" movement.

Hegel also believed that man's intellect was the highest manifestation of "God" in the universe and that man himself was involved in the dialectical process. Karl Marx (1818-1883) adopted the dialectical concept of progress but rejected Hegel's pantheism, formulating his own concept of "dialectical materialism" which became the philosophical basis for scientific socialism and communist revolution. If revolutionaries could harness the forces of the dialectical struggle, they could lead mankind into communist utopia. By viewing the dialectic as a scientifically provable force, like gravity, the communists saw themselves as a vanguard of social progress leading mankind into a glorious future.

Hegel also viewed the state as being "God" on earth, the ultimate authority and law in men's lives, because it represented man's collective power. It was this statist philosophy that set the stage for communism, socialism, Nazism, and two world wars. Ideas do indeed have consequences!

At Yale, the departure from Christian orthodoxy was begun in 1833 with the formation on campus of an American chapter of a German secret society known as The Order of Skull and Bones. Antony Sutton, in his book *America's Secret Establishment*, described The Order as a conspiracy to control the evolution of American society by putting its members in positions of leadership throughout the country:

> The Order is neither "left" nor "right." "Left" and "right" are artificial devices to bring about change, and the extremes of political left and political right are vital elements in a process of controlled change.... In the dialectical process a clash of opposites brings about a synthesis.... This conflict of opposites is essential to bring about change.... In the Hegelian system

conflict is essential. Furthermore, for Hegel and systems based on Hegel, the State is absolute. The State requires complete obedience from the individual citizen.... He finds freedom only in obedience to the State.

Sutton's hypothesis explains how such disparate personalities as William F. Buckley Jr., Robert Taft, and George Bush — all conservative Republicans — and William Sloane Coffin, John Kerry, and W. Averell Harriman — all liberal Democrats — could belong to the same secret society. It might also explain why William F. Buckley Jr. set out to destroy the influence of Robert Welch, founder of the John Birch Society, when the latter told the American people that there was a conspiracy of wealthy, well-placed Insiders who were controlling the course of events in America and the world.

Most interesting of all is how The Order has managed to gain control of American education. Three members of The Order were responsible for this development: Timothy Dwight (1849), professor at Yale Divinity School and later twelfth president of Yale; Daniel Coit Gilman (1852), first president of the University of California, first president of Johns Hopkins University, and first president of the Carnegie Institution; and Andrew Dickson White (1853), first president of Cornell and first president of the American Historical Association. All three also studied philosophy at the University of Berlin.

The three most important men in the progressive education movement — John Dewey, James McKeen Cattell, and G. Stanley Hall — were all at Johns Hopkins at the same time. Hall, who had studied Hegelianism at the University of Berlin and was trained by physiologist Wilhelm Wundt at Leipzig, taught Dewey and Cattell the new psychology. It was also at Johns Hopkins that Dewey was introduced to Hegelianism. James McKeen Cattell later studied under Wundt in Leipzig and went on to become America's leading educational psychologist at Teachers College, Columbia University. Dewey went on to create the new progressive curriculum for the public schools, which downgraded literacy and emphasized socialization. Cattell's reaction-time experiments in Wundt's laboratory were to become the "scientific" basis for getting rid of phonics and using the whole-word method for teaching children to read, which has become the cause of our reading problem and the dumbed-down curriculum in American public schools. Apparently, the dumbing down of the American people fits in very nicely with The Order's goal of producing a population that will obey the State and put up no resistance to the New World Order.

For the last sixty years or so, American education has been in the hands of humanists, socialists, and Hegelians turning out confused Americans who are not sure where they are going or why they are going there. But the secular State cannot accumulate total power because our Constitution stands in the way. It was written over two hundred years ago by men steeped in orthodox religion, who knew of man's depraved, sinful nature and were determined to make it as difficult as possible for evil men to gain total political power in the United States.

There was no such constitutional tradition in Germany to prevent Hitler from becoming a total dictator and leading a cultivated, civilized nation into utter depravity and ruin. The universities of Germany were spawning grounds for the ideas that led to Hitler, and they offered no resistance when he arrived on the scene. Why should they have resisted when he was basically what they wanted?

But the scene in America is different. We can prevent the rise of one big Hitler, but we have no way of preventing the many little Hitlers from occupying positions of power and influence in our many diverse institutions, public and private. The totalitarian spirit can be found in bureaucrats, judges, legislators, educators, labor unions, and corporate leaders. In fact, even with the demise of Soviet communism, we still have real-live, self-admitted totalitarians in the Communist Party USA, working with great dedication to turn America into a dictatorship of the proletariat, with plenty of sympathizers in our universities. One would think that the lessons of recent history would turn people away from such obvious insanity. However, Calvinists would simply remind us that man is innately depraved, a sinner to the core, attracted to evil to satisfy a variety of carnal and intellectual lusts.

For a time it seemed as if the establishment of major Catholic universities in America — Notre Dame, Loyola, Holy Cross, Boston

College, etc. — would offset the wholesale secularization of American higher education. Catholic educators offered some of the strongest arguments against progressive education. They vigorously defended the rights of parents and private schools. When the socialist Cardenas government in Mexico banned the operation of schools "directly or indirectly linked to any religious creed" in 1935, Msgr. Pascual Diaz, Archbishop of Mexico, instructed Catholics in a pastoral letter to refuse to comply with the new socialistic education laws:

> *First* – No Catholic can be a socialist, understanding by social-ism the philosophical, economic or social system which in one form or another does not recognize the rights of God and the church nor the natural right of every man to possess the goods he has acquired by his work or inherited legitimately, of which foments hatred and the unjust struggle of classes.
>
> *Second* – No Catholic can study or teach socialism, nor co-operate directly to those ends, since it contains many errors condemned by the church.
>
> *Third* – No Catholic can subscribe to declarations or formu-las according to which he approves, although only for appear-ance, socialistic education, since this would be to work against the dictates of his own conscience.
>
> *Fourth* – No Catholic can approve pedagogic naturalism or sexual education, since they are very grave errors which bring serious consequences.
>
> In saying that no Catholic can do what is prohibited, we make it clearly understood that those who do so commit a mortal sin.
>
> It should be understood that these prohibitions are not arbi-trary, but conform exactly with the general mandates of the church, which has the right, given by God Himself to com-mand its sons to do what is necessary for their eternal sal-vation and to prohibit them from doing what would carry them away from that end: proceeding in everything as a loving mother who seeks only the good of her children; when they work against what she commands, they bring down their own unhappiness.

That letter was not only signed by the Archbishop of Mexico, but by eight other archbishops and thirty bishops. It is doubtful that any Catholic archbishop would put his signature on that kind of letter today, for Catholic educators, with very few exceptions, have succumbed to the same secular humanist philosophy that now permeates all of academia.

A fundamentalist reaction has given rise to new institutions in which orthodox Biblical doctrines prevail. The founding of Bob Jones University, Regent University, Pensacola Christian College, Liberty University, and other schools indicates that God-centered education is still desired by a small but growing segment of the American population. But some day the humanist State may decide that God-centered education promotes religious bigotry and therefore must be eliminated.

Of course, freedom of religion is protected by the First Amendment to our Constitution. But that has not stopped the federal government from rescinding the tax-exempt status of Bob Jones University because of its rule against interracial dating. And it hasn't stopped school superintendents from harassing Christian homeschoolers for not complying with state education laws.

A new concept has emerged in our courts — the "state's compelling interest in education" — which is being deftly used by state prosecutors, school superintendents, and judges to override the constitutional guarantee of religious freedom. So far, no one has challenged that concept by asking the court or prosecutors to define what is meant by "education" or "compelling interest." Since education means different things to different people, how can the state have a compelling interest in something that no one agrees on? Progressives and traditionalists have profound disagreements when it comes to the aims and meaning of education.

With our great state universities all under humanist control, and our nation's public schools under similar control, it is obvious to anyone who can see, that under the guise of secularization the humanists have created the most powerful and pervasive government-funded establishment of religion that has ever existed in the United States.

Humanism is a religion. It is, in fact, Unitarianism in the guise of a secular philosophy. In 1987, U.S. District Court Judge W. Brevard Hand, in *Smith v. Board of School Commissioners of Mobile County, Alabama*, ruled that secular humanist philosophy is a religion. He wrote:

> For purposes of the First Amendment, secular humanism is a religious belief system, entitled to the protections of, and subject to the prohibitions of, the religion clauses.

Edwin H. Wilson, a Unitarian minister and one of the founders of the humanist movement, took great pains to show the interchangeability of humanism and Unitarianism in an article he wrote for the November-December 1962 issue of *The Humanist*. He stated:

> The American Humanist Association itself was organized...by a group composed primarily of liberal ministers and professors who were predominantly Unitarians and considered themselves as religious humanists.

> Of the thirty-four persons who signed the Humanist Manifesto in 1933, all but four can be readily identified as "religious humanists."... My conviction is that a probe into what is actually believed would show that the "liberal Unitarian position" and what is generally presented as Humanism — whether as a religion or as a philosophy — differ very little.

Then there was the Torcaso case, in which the Supreme Court recognized Buddhism, Taoism, Ethical Culture, and Secular Humanism as religions existing in the United States even though they do not teach what is traditionally considered belief in God.

There is no doubt that our government education system is an illegal establishment of religion in flagrant violation of our Constitution. The American people permit this system to exist mainly because of ignorance, confusion, and deference to a number of powerful and corrupt special interests. But a nation that prefers to live with lies — because it is too cowardly and corrupt to fight for the truth — will have to suffer the consequences of its depravity.

THE AMERICAN DIALECTIC

The dialectic that drives American politics was quite visible on the platform at George W. Bush's inauguration. To the left of the Bushes sat the socialists and Gramscian commies: Bill, who burned eighty-or-so men, women, and children at Waco and handed Elian over to Castro; his sulking partner, Al Gore, whose family owes much of its wealth to Kremlin agent Armand Hammer; and Chris Dodd, senator from Connecticut who spent years defending the Sandinista communists of Nicaragua. They held the White House for eight years, and now their reign was over. Just to have survived them is an achievement for any conservative.

On their right was George W. Bush, born-again Christian, basically conservative; Dick Cheney, one of the most conservative men who ever sat in Congress; and a whole lot of other people on the side of the Aisles. Both ministers, Franklin Graham who gave the invocation and the black minister from Houston who gave the benediction, invoked the name of Jesus Christ at the close of their prayers. President Bush took the oath of office with his hand on the Bible. His address had the spiritual tone associated with our religious heritage. After eight years of Clinton debauchery, it was quite a change. Even the presence of the chief justice of the Supreme Court administering the oath had symbolic meaning. It was he who brought the dispute over the vote count in Florida to an end, affirming Bush's victory.

This was a peaceful moment in the ongoing revolution, a brief moment of rest. The system demands it. Although the dialectic is the ongoing, endless conflict between the two philosophies of life and government, there are rules whereby the two sides conduct themselves. Clinton is always trying to stretch the rules, thus his farewell speech was really a critique of the new Bush administration. He's a dialectician down to his fingernails.

The new president didn't spend his time criticizing the Clinton administration. He thanked Clinton for his service to the nation. Bush plays by the rules, and he does so graciously. He won in Florida even though the mobs shouting insults at him during the parade didn't think so. They are also part of the dialectic, the more ugly part. Conservative citizens act differently. They brush up on their Second Amendment rights.

What is the dialectic? It is the means by which the far Left moves our society slowly but inexorably in its direction — toward socialism. The dialectical process was conceived in the early nineteenth century by German philosopher, Georg Wilhelm Friedrich Hegel (1770–1831), a pantheist, who believed in a world soul that was using the dialectical process to achieve its own perfection. Since the human race was part of the world soul, our history was also part of this ongoing dialectical process, or conflict, between the thesis and the antithesis to form a new synthesis, which then becomes the new thesis. Karl Marx (1818-1883) junked the spiritual aspect of Hegel's dialectic, and attached it to a purely materialistic, godless view of the universe — hence the creation of "dialectical materialism," the process whereby the human race inches toward communism.

In American politics, the dialecticians of the Left view the thesis as the conservative status quo, the antithesis as the socialists and communists opposing the status quo, and the synthesis as the new status quo after the conservatives have compromised and moved toward the Left. That is why no conservative administration has been able to undo any of the liberal programs and why our federal and state governments keep growing in power and scope, imposing more and more restrictions on American freedom.

A case in point is the Department of Education, which was established by liberals in the Carter administration. Attempts by conservatives to close it down have been thwarted time and again until conservatives have become resigned to its continued existence. What prevents Republicans from breaking the dialectical cycle is their lack of understanding of how it works and their lack of courage. Politics is supposed to be the art of compromise. But with the dialectic at work, compromise means surrender on the installment plan.

The Bible, of course, teaches absolutes, for there are no dialectical compromises possible with God's law. You may disobey His law, but you can't change it. That is also true of our Declaration of

Independence and the U.S. Constitution. Although the Left would like to get rid of them, the best they can do is dialectically tear them apart. It is only the vigilance of patriotic gun owners who have prevented the complete destruction of the Second Amendment.

The control of public opinion by the Left is an important factor in the dialectical process. The Left, because it controls the mass media, has a tremendously powerful force on its side. If a conservative president tried to close down the Department of Education, the mass media would rise up with a barrage of criticism that would send conservative legislators to their bomb shelters. Many parents, willing pawns of the dialecticians, would rise up in anger against those members of Congress who would dare to close down the department.

The leftists are very good at using the mob. They actually train mob agitators. I remember when I was a student at the City College of New York in the late 1940s how the communists organized a student strike over a professor they didn't like, and the students marched around like sheep, mesmerized by the self-appointed student leaders who were all communists and trained in the arts of agitprop.

The "protestors" at the Inauguration Parade were a leftist rent-a-mob. There's an outfit in Philadelphia that professionally organizes mob demonstrations. They have to be well organized if they are going to make their impact on the six o'clock or eleven o'clock news. They need signs, slogans, transportation, food, lodging, etc. The leftists do it up brown because that's their *métier*, their profession, and they know how to make use of the TV cameras. No cameras, no mobs.

Conservatives make lousy mobs, but they can make the rounds of their legislators in a civilized way to influence their actions. But when the right-to-lifers demonstrated on January 22 in Washington, they got TV coverage because the demonstration was large, colorful, and orderly, and President Bush had just cancelled U.S. taxpayer funding for abortions in foreign countries.

Not all compromise is dialectic. There are many instances in which compromise is warranted. But compromise is not warranted where it violates a conservative's stand on Biblical absolutes. George H. W. Bush turned his promise to a lie by reneging on his pledge not to raise taxes. That compromise cost him much conservative support and lost him a second term. He listened to his Harvard dialectician, Richard Darman, who believed that the purpose of government was to move the nation forward — not saying what was meant by forward.

Of course, the dialectic doesn't always work in the leftists' favor. Thus their philosophy calls for taking one step back, whenever necessary, in order to take two steps forward later. In dress parades, the Red Army in China actually takes two steps forward and one step back, demonstrating the communist dialectic at work. I'm sure that Clinton and his Gramscian buddies are not at all fazed by having to take the one step back with Bush's election, because in their hearts they are certain that the next big dialectical move will be two steps forward.

In political terms, the dialectic conflict is between two visions of government: the original vision of the Founding Fathers of a representative republic with a Constitution that limits the power of government at all levels, and the leftist vision of a social democracy in which government power is unlimited. A constitutional republic is better than a social democracy because it protects us from the tyranny of men. Since the agenda of a Gore presidency would have just about destroyed our constitutional republic, the conservatives on the U.S. Supreme Court decided to use their power to prevent Gore from overturning the Bush victory. They checkmated the dialectic.

OUR LOBOTOMIZED CHILDREN

You see them everywhere. These young people without brains who congregate in parking lots, haunt shopping malls, and drive around aimlessly on Saturday night, partying, drinking, smoking, having sex, experimenting with drugs, getting into fights. They complain so often about being bored, bored in school, bored with themselves, bored with life. Of course, the reason why they are bored is because they themselves are so utterly boring. They haven't read a good book in their entire lives; they have no intellectual interests or curiosity. It's as if the entire world of the mind is closed to them, and the only activities that make them feel alive are uncontrolled sex, drugs, and violence — all of which are so self-destructive.

Jay Leno often interviews these vapid individuals on the avenues of Los Angeles so that we can get a good laugh from their ignorance. But their ignorance is nothing to laugh about. It's a great American tragedy. We compel these kids to spend twelve years in school at a cost of billions of dollars to be "educated," and what we get is appalling ignorance. It's as if all of these kids have undergone lobotomies, so that they no longer have minds that can analyze, or think, or be creative. What we have are teenage consumers, easily stimulated by highly emotional ads, whose interests are limited to what they can touch in a department store or see in the movies or on television or hear on a rap music station.

Back in the 1930s and '40s, when I was going to school, I was never bored. I could read, and therefore the library was a tremendous source of stimulating ideas and stories. The world was a tremendously interesting place. I was taught music appreciation in the third grade by a teacher who played short classics on a portable Victrola. That short once-a-week class opened the whole world of classical music for me. I can still remember some of the pieces she played: "The Swan" by Saint-Saens, "March Slav" by Tchaikovsky, "The William Tell Overture" by Rossini.

I read good poetry written by the great poets, not the cute greeting-card type of poems that kids now read, devoid of insight or wisdom or true beauty of language and thought. And it isn't that today's kids are not capable of learning to enjoy such great literature. It's that their limited ability to read makes it impossible for them to even venture into that ever fascinating and expansive world of the written word.

Some months ago, a father brought his fifteen-year-old, ninth-grade son to me to be tested. This very intelligent boy had a reading problem that was preventing him from advancing in his education. He was tested by the school, which determined that the boy should sit closer to the teacher, be given extra time to "process information," have his assignments cut into smaller segments for easier handling, listen to books on tapes, use Cliff notes when reading novels, and stay after school to make up for missed work. There was no attempt whatever to deal with the boy's reading problem. Which is why his father brought him to me. I cure dyslexics.

This youngster was no different from so many others I have worked with over the last thirty years. He was a typical sight-reader who had been given a sight vocabulary to memorize in the first grade and thereby acquired a holistic reflex, which would handicap him for the rest of his life. In other words, he had been taught to look at each word as if it were a Chinese character and was required to remember it holistically by its configuration or association with a picture. When a child is taught to read holistically and develops a holistic reflex, the reflex becomes an obstacle to seeing the word in its phonetic structure, especially if the child has been taught little or no phonics.

All alphabetically written words have a phonetic structure. But you must learn the letter sounds and be drilled in consonant-vowel combinations in order to develop the needed phonetic reflex or automaticity, so that reading becomes easy and enjoyable and the phonetic structure of a word is perfectly transparent. But if you have not been taught intensive phonics, and were made to look at each word as a picture, you will never become a fluent reader.

When I asked this boy, who is now in high school, what was a short *a*, he had no idea. He did understand the concept that letters stand for sounds. But this kind of phonetic knowledge in and of itself does not create a phonetic reflex; it simply provides information, which the child may or may not use. And because it requires conscious effort to use this information, reading becomes a difficult and painful chore that must be avoided. In fact, I once tutored an adult, a highly successful entrepreneur, who told me that he would rather be beaten than have to read.

This could easily have become the case with this youngster. When I had him read paragraphs from a variety of books, it was easy to see that he was a holistic reader and made all of the misreadings typical of this kind of sight-reader. The only way he could read multisyllabic words was to find smaller sight words within the big words. But he made so many crucial errors in his reading that his comprehension had to suffer.

That the schools permit these learning problems to persist and can offer no hope of meaningful remediation means that every child who has developed a holistic reflex is condemned to a life with a very limited use of mind. It is true that some individuals have the inner resources to overcome their reading disability, but apparently these empty-headed kids with the lobotomized look do not have that inner resource. They will go through life believing that they are stupid, pursuing careers that require a minimum of reading, and leading lives of illiteracy. They will suffer, their children will suffer, and America will suffer.

Some months ago, *Frontline*, of the Public Broadcasting System, did a documentary program on the "Lost Children of Conyers, Georgia," where an outbreak of syphilis among high school students brought attention to the dissolute lifestyle of many of the teenagers in that town. The social life of these kids revolved around their peer groups at school. They were bored. They had nothing to do, so they indulged in sex, drinking, drugs, cigarettes, and obscene rap music. What was missing was the life of the mind, the ability to think, to analyze, to understand that life meant more than just abusing oneself. Everybody tended to blame the parents because the parents gave these kids every material good available.

Nobody blamed the school and the fact that these kids had

been lobotomized in the first grade by their loving teachers. These kids could not use their minds because they no longer had them. Their lives would revolve around emotional and sensual activities that resembled a roller coaster ride. They would be reduced to primitive pre-civilized behavior. True, they had all of the paraphernalia of our high-tech civilization, but their emotional lives would be lived on the level of preliterate, prehistoric society.

That's what public education has given us, and the vast majority of Americans have no idea why it is the way it is. And that's why they keep supporting the system with billions of tax dollars.

Fortunately, there are a growing number of parents who have seen the light and have turned to homeschooling. In general, homeschoolers teach their children to read by phonics so that their children can eventually educate themselves by reading history, biographies, novels, poetry, and the Bible.

Meanwhile, the two major candidates for the presidency offer different approaches to our ongoing educational problems. Gore, the obedient child of the National Education Association, strongly opposes vouchers and is not at all friendly toward homeschoolers. In fact the Democratic Party platform reflects the NEA's hostility toward homeschooling. Bush, on the other hand, favors vouchers, speaks highly of phonics, and is sympathetic toward homeschooling.

Both, of course, intend to spend lots more money on public education. What this means is that we ought not to expect politicians to solve our education problems. They will have to be solved by parents willing to make the necessary sacrifices to send their children to decent private schools or educate them at home, for the only true reform of education will take place when the government gets out of the education business.

WHEN TEACHERS BECOME PSYCHOTHERAPISTS

Most parents of public school children are unaware that teachers all across America are now practicing psychotherapy in the classroom without a license. Not only do they not have a license, but they haven't even had adequate training. In fact, many teachers don't even know that they are practicing psychotherapy. They think that what they are doing has something to do with education. For example, sex education, death education, drug education, decision making, transcendental meditation, sensitivity training, values clarification, and other such programs are now considered a legitimate and important part of education. But they are not. They are forms of psychotherapy intended to affect the emotions, beliefs, values, and behavior of the students.

All of this is very well explained in a booklet of forty-nine pages, which I recently received from the Commonwealth Education Organization. The booklet, written by Dr. Ann Landell, clinical psychologist, is entitled, *Shifting Roles*. It deals with the heavy-handed intrusion of psychotherapy into education, which has turned students, who supposedly go to school to acquire certain academic skills, into patients whose emotions and values become the school's major concerns.

Dr. Landell asks three basic questions, which she answered in the booklet: (1) How do the professions of psychology and education differ? (2) Do all children need therapy in the same way that all children need reading, writing, science, and math? (3) Does the practice of classroom psychology always help children, or can it harm them?

There is no doubt that there is a big difference between education and psychology. When I went to school back in the 1930s and '40s, teachers taught academic subject matter exclusively. My teachers were not in the least interested in my feelings, or beliefs, or values.

83

They only wanted to know if I was learning what they were teaching. I was a student, not a patient. As a result, those of us who attended school in those years came out of the system pretty well educated. We fought in World War II and won, and many of my colleagues went on to build the foundations of what is today our high-tech economy. Tom Brokaw has called us the best generation in American history, all because we knew how to read and write, defended the U.S. Constitution, and adhered to Biblical moral principles.

Psychologists deal with mental and behavioral disorders. They deal with deviants from the norm and therefore require highly specialized training. Teachers are supposedly trained to teach children academic skills and a body of significant knowledge. The children they teach are generally considered normal. But behavioral scientists have targeted normal children as those requiring radical change. All you have to do is read Professor Benjamin Bloom's definition of education in his *Taxonomy of Educational Objectives* — the bible of progressive curriculum developers published in 1956 — to understand where this intrusive concept of psychology comes from.

Bloom wrote:

> By educational objectives, we mean explicit formulations of the ways in which students are expected to be changed by the educative process. That is, the ways in which they will change in their thinking, their feelings, and their actions....

> (Psychologist Gordon) Allport (1954) emphasizes the basic reorganization that must take place in the individual if really new values and character traits are to be formed....

> The evidence points out convincingly to the fact that age is a factor operating against attempts to effect a complete or thoroughgoing reorganization of attitudes and values....

> The evidence collected thus far suggests that a single hour of classroom activity under certain conditions may bring about a major reorganization in cognitive as well as affective behaviors.

The behavioral psychologists divided education into two domains: cognitive and affective. The cognitive domain supposedly dealt with academic instruction, while the affective domain was the cover under which psychotherapy was to be introduced into the classroom. Note that the aim of effecting a "complete or thoroughgoing reorganization of attitudes and values" implied that the attitudes and values of the normal child had to be changed. These were values, often religious, that the child had acquired at home from his parents.

Charlotte Iserbyt, author of *The Deliberate Dumbing Down of America*, wrote in her preface:

> I have always found it interesting that the controversial school programs are the only ones that have the word "education" attached to them! I don't recall — until recently — "math ed.," "reading ed.," "history ed.," or "science ed." A good rule of thumb ... is to question any subject that has the word "education" attached to it.

To prove her point, Iserbyt quoted from *The School Counselor* of May 1977, which dealt with the subject of death education:

> An underlying, but seldom spoken, assumption of much of the death education movement is that Americans handle death and dying poorly and that we ought to be doing better at it. As in the case of many other problems, many Americans believe that education can initiate change. Change is evident, and death education will play as important a part in changing attitudes toward death as sex education played in changing attitudes toward sex information and wider acceptance of various sexual practices.

Which means that when they teach "sex education," they are really just teaching sex. When they teach "drug education," they are really teaching drugs. But even the so-called cognitive domain has been contaminated with psychotherapy through the use of bibliotherapy. Dr. Landell wrote:

> Bibliotherapy, as the word implies, is a method of doing therapy through books.... [For example]: Third graders studying slavery spend one day as master and one day as slave in the classroom. What did the children learn from this intense les-

son? After "feeling the pain" of being a slave to classmates relishing their master role as only third graders can, one child said, "It's really important to be top dog!" Creating committed overlords was not the intent of the lesson, but it was the result. If you spent a day as slave and a day as overlord, which would you choose? And choose with gusto, because of the emotionally manipulative teaching method.

Emotional manipulation is used throughout the curriculum to produce politically correct young adults who may not know how to read, but will know how to respond correctly to an assortment of stimuli. If the young adult does not have the intellectual, psychological, philosophical, or theological maturity to deal with the stimuli thrown at him, he will respond emotionally, like any primitive, superstitious individual.

On the matter of decision making, Dr. Landell wrote:

Decision making models used in sex education, drug, and suicide prevention programs often lead children to list the pros and cons of these actions. Each pro listed whets the appetite for the action, stirs interest and creates motivation for the action. As one sixth grader said to her father, "Daddy, you better get me out of that DARE program. It makes drugs look interesting." ...Weighing the pros and cons of such behaviors changes them in students' minds from "weirdness out there" to "things I could do."

Dr. Landell also discusses the psychotherapeutic issues of Self-Esteem Education, Higher-Order Thinking, Dual Roles, and Confidentiality. If you have a child in a public school, you owe it to yourself to get hold of this booklet. You can do so by writing: Commonwealth Education Organization, 90 Beta Drive, Pittsburgh, PA 15238, or phone: 412-967-9691, or fax: 412-967-9694.

THE WAR BETWEEN HUMANISM AND CHRISTIANITY EXAMINED IN *THE MESSIANIC CHARACTER OF AMERICAN EDUCATION*

There is no doubt that Rev. Rousas J. Rushdoony has done more to advance the cause of educational freedom in America than any other Christian theologian. His classic study, *The Messianic Character of American Education*, first published in 1963 and recently reissued by Ross House Books, is a monument to independent scholarship and historical investigation. In that book we see clearly delineated the philosophical conflict between humanism and Christianity that has been raging for decades throughout American culture and particularly in the field of education.

That humanism not only threatens Christian education but educational freedom in general is well demonstrated by the link Rev. Rushdoony shows existing between religious liberty and educational freedom, for education is basically a religious function, even when it is atheistic, and Christian education is hardly viable without religious freedom. As Rev. Rushdoony wrote in *Roots of Reconstruction* (p. 11):

> Among Nietzsche's manuscripts, after his death, was found a slip of paper on which he had written these words: "Since the old God has been abolished, I am prepared to rule the world." This is the meaning of humanism's inescapable totalitarianism. Total government is a necessity, and everything in man requires it. If there is no god to provide it, then man must supply it….

87

> In the United States, the efforts of federal and state govern-
> ments to control churches and Christian Schools are the
> logical results of their humanism. There must be sovereignty
> and law, and [that] it must be man's, not God's, is their faith.
> Clearly, we are in the basic religious war, and there can be no
> compromise nor negotiation in this war. Humanism seeks to
> abolish the God of Scripture and rule the world.

In America, the aims of humanism can only be achieved through the
control of children and their education. The ultimate issue, therefore,
is the ownership of children. Rev. Rushdoony wrote (Ibid., p. 10):

> The first and basic premise of paganism, socialism, and Molech
> worship is the claim that the state owns the child. The basic
> premise of the public schools is this claim of ownership, a fact
> some parents are encountering in the courts. It is the essence
> of paganism to claim first the lives of the children, then the
> properties of the people.

Thus, religious and educational freedom essentially rest on the foundation of God's ownership. In the end, the issue of Christian liberty can only be resolved in a philosophical confrontation between
Christians and the state, the result of which must be the restoration
of genuine religious liberty if this country is to remain faithful to its
original conception. Rev. Rushdoony wrote:

> The church and the Christian School are not the property of
> the state, nor are they the property of the congregation: they
> are the Lord's, and can be surrendered to no man.

The principle of God's ownership was implicitly understood by the
Founding Fathers who wrote the U.S. Constitution and upheld God's
sovereignty over man. As long as the civil government remained
subsidiary to God's sovereignty, it was legitimate and thereby sup-
portable by Christians. But the introduction of secular, government-
owned and controlled schools and colleges began to erode that basic
understanding in the minds of the American people. Hegel's statist
philosophy, with its pagan-inspired pantheism, slowly absorbed the
loyalty of the academic elite so that the state, in Hegel's words, became "God walking on earth."

Slowly but surely the concept of religious freedom gave way to that of religious toleration. Religious freedom had meant that the state had no jurisdiction over the church, its schools, or its affairs. But the new doctrine of religious toleration meant that the state granted certain privileges to churches and religious schools at its own pleasure, privileges, such as tax exemption, which could be withdrawn at any time for some "compelling state interest." Rev. Rushdoony wrote (Ibid., p. 150):

> The fact is that religious liberty is dead and buried; it needs to be resurrected. We cannot begin to cope with our present crisis until we recognize that religious liberty has been replaced with religious toleration....
>
> We may be able to live under religious toleration, but it will beget all the ancient evils of compromise, hypocrisy, and a purely or largely public religion. It will replace conscience with a state license, and freedom with a state-endowed cell of narrow limits. This is the best that toleration may afford us in the days ahead.

The simple fact is that we already have a public, government-ordained religion. It is called humanism, and its most popular festival is Halloween, which is of pagan, Druidic origin. Today, it is lavishly and nauseatingly celebrated in all of the public schools of America as one of the many insidious means now being used by government educators to paganize or de-Christianize American children.

However, Rev. Rushdoony's most noteworthy contribution to the heated debate over educational jurisdiction is his profound analysis of the central role of the family in Christian society as based on Biblical principles. He wrote (Ibid., p. 35):

> In Scripture, the family is the basic institution of society, to whom all the most basic powers are given, save one: the death penalty. (Hence, the death penalty could not be executed on Cain.) The family is man's basic government, his best school, and his best church....
>
> To review briefly the basic powers which Scripture gives to the family, the first is the control of children. The control of chil-

dren is the control of the future. This power belongs neither to church nor state, nor to the school, but only to the family....

Second, power over property is given in Scripture to the family.... God gives control of property into the hands of the family, not the state, nor the individual....

Third, inheritance in Scripture is exclusively a family power, governed by God's law....

Fourth, welfare is the responsibility of the family, beginning with the care of its own.

Fifth, education, a basic power, is given by God to the family as its power and responsibility. The modern state claims the right to control and provide education, and it challenges the powers of the family in this area also....

Humanistic statism sees control of the child and the family as basic to its drive towards totalitarianism.

Even though Rushdoony's words were written in 1979, we see the accuracy of that analysis in the federal government's recent enactment of Goals 2000 and the enactment in various states of Outcome Based Education, which calls for greater and greater state intrusion into family life. The extensive data-collection projects of the National Center for Education Statistics will give bureaucrats the intimate private information needed to impose government control over children and families.

Since the aim of humanistic education is not to educate in the traditional sense, but to change the beliefs, values, and behavior of the students, behavioral scientists have emerged as the true developers of the American school curriculum. Their aim has been to transform the American public school into a humanist parochial school, and they have devoted years to developing the necessary means to bring this about. One of the basic tenets of behaviorism is that the younger the child, the easier it is to change his values. Professor Benjamin Bloom, the godfather of Outcome Based Education, wrote in 1956 in his famous *Taxonomy of Educational Objectives* (p. 58):

The evidence points out convincingly to the fact that age is a factor operating against attempts to effect a complete or thorough-going reorganization of attitudes and values....

The evidence collected thus far suggests that a single hour of classroom activity under certain conditions may bring about a major reorganization in cognitive as well as affective domains. We are of the opinion that this will prove to be a most fruitful area of research in connection with the affective domain. (p. 58)

Forty years later, the research has been completed, and the programs are now in the schools! Note the presumption of the psycho-educators that they have the right to reorganize the attitudes and values of the children without their parents' knowledge or consent. But according to Scripture, as Rev. Rushdoony makes quite clear, the family has the responsibility for the education of its children, not the agents of the state.

As a champion of educational freedom, Rev. Rushdoony was a pioneer in the advocacy of homeschooling because he recognized that there can be no educational freedom without the family taking full responsibility for the education of its children. He testified in various courts throughout America at more hearings and trials involving homeschoolers than any other Christian leader, and his testimony helped clarify the legal and philosophical issues involved. The Christian homeschooling family is of particular significance because it has made a complete break with the humanist institutions of the state. This is surely a revolutionary act because it rejects the power of the state to impose its will on the Christian family.

There is no doubt that the decline of Christianity in America is due to the capture of its educational institutions by the humanists. The process started as early as 1805 when the Unitarians took control of Harvard University and began their long-range campaign to eradicate Calvinism as the chief spiritual and cultural force in America. Rev. Rushdoony wrote (*Messianic Character*, p. 333):

The Messianic Utopianism of early educators often took extravagant form, as claims were made that prisons, crime, sin, war, tyranny, and every form of evil and disharmony would

disappear with the triumph of universal statist education....
Although other churches made their contributions to the
movement ... it was Unitarianism in particular which gave
itself wholeheartedly to the cause of messianic education and
statism. The influence of that church on nineteenth century
America is too seldom appreciated.... Institutional Unitarianism under-rated itself because it had a marginal doctrine
of the church; it sought "establishment," in a very real sense,
in and through the schools, and the schools became the em-
bodiment and establishment of Unitarian faith in salvation by
statist education.

Rev. Rushdoony amply documents all of this in *The Messianic Character of American Education* by providing insightful biographical studies
of the major individuals who transformed American education from
its God-centered origins to its present atheist-humanist philosophy.
He examines the lives of such luminaries in the pantheon of public
education as Horace Mann, Henry Barnard, Nicholas Murray Butler,
G. Stanley Hall, J. B. Watson, Edward L. Thorndike, John Dewey,
and others. All of these "educators" had one thing in common: they
rejected Christ as the true Messiah and created a new messianic vision based on science, evolution, and psychology, the chief apostles
of which were Darwin, Marx, and Freud. A reading of this book
alone should convince any Christian that America's secular educational institutions are the primary cause of the nation's moral and
spiritual decline — aided and abetted by a decadent entertainment
industry. That is why an exodus by Christians from these institutions
and the creation of new God-centered institutions is imperative if
America is to be restored to its moral and spiritual health.

Although some atheist humanists deny that their philosophy,
or worldview, constitutes a religion, other humanists are quite ready
to proclaim humanism as a religion. In fact, the Humanist Manifesto
of 1933 was written by young Unitarian ministers as an expression
of their creed. Proof of this can be found in *The Humanist* itself, the
official publication of the humanist movement.

The forerunner of *The Humanist* was *The New Humanist*,
which first appeared in 1928 as a monthly bulletin of the Humanist

Fellowship, an organization formed by Unitarian students from the University of Chicago and its related theological schools. Its early editors — Harold Buschman, Edwin H. Wilson, and Raymond B. Bragg — were young Unitarian ministers. It was on the initiatives of Bragg that the drafting of a Humanist Manifesto (1933) was begun. Professor Roy Wood Sellars wrote the first draft. The Manifesto appeared in the April 1933 issue of *The New Humanist*. In an article entitled "Humanism as a Religion," published in *The Humanist* (Vol. 1, 1941, p. 5), Sellars wrote:

> Undeniably there is something imaginative and daring in bringing together in one phrase two such profoundly symbolic words as humanism and religion. An intimate union is foreshadowed in which religion will become humanistic and humanism religious. And I believe that such a synthesis is imperative if humanity is ever to achieve a firm and adequate understanding of itself and its cosmic situation....

> To the thoughtful of our day, humanism is being offered as this kind of a religion, a religion akin to science and philosophy and yet not a mere abstract of these specialized endeavors.... Religious humanism rests upon the bedrock of a decision that it is, in the long run, saner and wiser to face facts than to live in a world of fable.

In November 1962, Edwin H. Wilson wrote in *The Humanist*:

> Of the thirty-four persons who signed the Humanist Manifesto in 1933, all but four can be readily identified as "religious humanists" who considered Humanism as the development of a better and truer religion and as the next step ahead for those who sought it.

In June 1951, Wilson wrote:

> Today, I am suggesting that there is in the world as a present and potent faith, embraced by vast numbers, yet seldom mentioned — a fourth faith — namely Humanism.

And in *The Humanist* of 1954 (Vol. 15, No. 4, p. 180) we read:

> Since humanism appears as a genuinely living option for many
> people, especially among students, teachers, and intellectuals
> generally, it may be appropriately studied as a religion. Indeed,
> it is not unfair to call it the fourth main religious option, along
> with Judaism, Roman Catholicism, and Protestantism, for
> thoughtful men in the contemporary Western world.

Humanism is, for many humanists, a religion on a par with other religions. And that is why the war between humanism and Christianity
can be viewed as nothing but a religious war declared by humanists
on Christianity. The Manifesto of 1933 states:

> Religious humanism maintains that all associations and insti-
> tutions exist for the fulfillment of human life. The intelligent
> evaluation, transformation, control, and direction of such as-
> sociations and institutions with a view to the enhancement of
> human life is the purpose and program of humanism. Cer-
> tainly religious institutions, their ritualistic forms, ecclesiasti-
> cal methods, and communal activities must be reconstituted
> as rapidly as experience allows, in order to function effectively
> in the modern world.

In other words, the humanist program calls for taking control of and
transforming all of the cultural and religious institutions and associations of the nation so that they will be made to advance effectively
the humanist agenda. No other religion in America calls for taking
over the institutions and associations of other religions. We are supposed to be living in a society where religious freedom is respected by
all religions. But we have it in the words of the Humanist Manifesto
itself: the intention of humanists to reconstitute everybody else's religions, rituals, and ecclesiastical practices to conform with humanist
goals.

That is why the humanists have no qualms about imposing
their religious beliefs on all the children in the public schools, regardless of the different religions of the parents. Clearly the humanists are violating the constitutional prohibition against a government
establishment of religion. But they are so strongly motivated by their
messianic fervor, that the objections of Christians to the humanist

agenda is dismissed as censorship, intolerance, paranoia, or insanity.

Speaking of insanity, the summer 1993 issue of the secular humanist magazine *Free Inquiry* published a series of articles under the heading "Is Religion a Form of Insanity?" One of the articles, "The Mental Health of Atheists" by John F. Schumaker, seemed to prove just the opposite. He wrote:

> If we define mental health in the traditional way as the absence of psychopathological symptoms, then we see that religion does tend to act in the service of mental health. The reverse is true when one defines mental health in terms of more humanistic concepts, such as autonomous functioning, rationality, cognitive flexibility, and the like....
>
> Recently I edited a book titled *Religion and Mental Health....* My own chapter ... concentrates on the mental health consequences of atheism. There, I refer to my research showing atheists to have forty-five percent more symptoms of psychological disturbance than their strongly religious counterparts....
>
> ... I managed to find three other studies that approximated an acceptable assessment of mental health in decidedly irreligious people. Coincidentally, two of them used the same test that I used in my above-mentioned study, namely the Langer Symptom Survey Scale (LSS)....
>
> One study found the irreligious sample to have eighty-five percent more symptoms as measured by LSS (Crawford, Handal, and Weiner, 1989, *Review of Religious Research*, Vol. 31, 16–22). That research team also found that irreligious people showed themselves to be significantly less psychologically well-adjusted as measured by tests of life satisfaction and social adjustment. In a different study, using only women as subjects, irreligious people had sixty-three percent more LSS symptoms than highly religious people (Handal, Black-Lopez, and Moergen, 1989, *Psychological Reports*, Vol. 65, 971–975). Therefore, three similar studies, using the same mental health index, found irreligion to be associated with considerably more symptoms of psychopathology.

In a different type of study, irreligious individuals were compared to their religious counterparts on the extent to which they felt that "life is worth living" (Hadaway and Roof, 1978, *Review of Religious Research*, vol. 19, 297–307). People for whom religion was extremely important found their lives significantly more "worthwhile." It is interesting that people with low or medium intensity religion fared no better than those with no religion at all. This was also found in two previously mentioned studies. So it may be, as some thinkers have speculated, that weak or ambivalent religion only serves to upset people. The real psychological benefits of religion may be reserved for those who embrace religion wholeheartedly.

Sometimes it pays to read secular humanist literature! You'd think that Dr. Schumaker's researches would have turned him into a religionist. Alas, such is not the case. Concluding his article, he wrote:

> If religion is generally beneficial to psychological health, that is unfortunate.... While I agree with [Paul] Kurtz that it is possible to live without religion, I suggest that most people find such a road to be psychologically bumpy. As long as it feels so good to succumb to the transcendental temptation, I fear that religion will live on as our "murderous god of health," a term Peter Shaffer used in *Equus* to describe "normality," a related curse.

Therefore, according to Dr. Schumaker, people believe in religion because it makes them feel good and thereby enhances their mental health. But the research shows that only deeply religious people derive psychological benefits from religion. Those with low or medium religious beliefs feel just as bad as atheists, probably because they are full of doubt and inner conflict. This should explain why the orthodox are so well adjusted to the real world and so well focused when it comes to such matters as homeschooling. No doubt this is why they are so greatly feared by secular humanists and the lukewarmers.

Concerning the future, Rev. Rushdoony offered this optimistic view (p. 332):

> The future has never been shaped by majorities but rather by dedicated minorities. And free men do not wait for the future;

they create it. The difficulties and problems in that venture are to them not a hindrance but a challenge that must be met. Those critics of the schools who wait for the state or society to act work on the same premise of the primacy of the group. The futility of their cause is thus foreordained. Free men do not look to the state for the opportunities and results of freedom.

That is why the homeschool movement represents the essence and best hope of a free society in which individual families decide freely how to educate their own children. Its growth is the best indicator that "free men do not wait for the future; they create it."

VALUES AND PUBLIC EDUCATION: THE CULTURAL CIVIL WAR

There is a myth extant among a significant body of educators in America that a teacher can be value-neutral in the classroom. A corollary to that myth is the notion that a teacher must not impose his own set of values on the students and that the students must be free to develop their own values. The process whereby this takes place is known as values clarification — the means whereby the student works out or discovers his own set of values based on his desires, experiences, beliefs, and inner personal instincts.

The first question that arises from this view is, how is it possible for any living human being to be value-neutral? Indeed, what does value-neutral mean? In classroom practice it has meant bringing up moral issues for discussion among the students with the teacher remaining mute, refusing to interject his views. Somehow, it was expected that through the enlightening process of clarification, the students would arrive at a suitable personal moral code, all by themselves, without adult guidance.

Now there is something obviously suspect in such an idea. Why bring up the subject of morals in a class if the teacher is not going to teach morality? Would that same teacher decide to bring up the subject of World War II and remain mute, while the students in their ignorance discussed it? The implication is that you can teach history, but you cannot teach morals. Children must discover them for themselves.

Can children come up with a well-thought-out personal set of values merely through a rap session on moral issues? I hardly think so, for the simple reason that children have simply not lived long enough or experienced enough to understand the serious ramifications of their naive, juvenile decision making. If this is what ordinary common sense tells us, then why do educators expect children to

99

accomplish in a few classroom rap sessions what the world's greatest philosophers have been unable to do in a couple of thousand years?

Obviously, a child comes to school with some idea of values. After all, a child learns very early in life what's important to him and what is not. But the child doesn't use the term values, which is really a philosophical abstraction.

What is a value? According to my *New World Dictionary of the American Language*, it is that quality of a thing according to which it is thought of as being more or less desirable, useful, estimable, important, worthy of esteem for its own sake.

We generally think of values in economic terms. Something that's expensive is considered of high value and is termed dear. The British sum up capitalism in four words: buy cheap, sell dear. Note how loaded these words are. *Cheap* not only connotes low price but also shoddy merchandise. It also connotes low morals: a cheap trick, a cheap thrill. *Dear* connotes high price as well as emotional value: a dear friend, a dear mother.

Children learn about values in emotional terms. Parents are dear because they are a source of love, without which the child cannot survive. When children were asked in a survey what they wanted most, the answer was more time with their parents. And so children learn at home what is dear and what is not. They also learn that in matters of clothes, food, entertainment, etc., they have their likes and dislikes. Values, or tastes, are personal. *De gustibus non est disputandum*. There is no arguing over tastes.

The idea that an educator can be value-neutral is, of course, a sham. One has to be dead to be value-neutral. The very condition of being alive requires value judgment if one is to survive. The body itself, from the moment of conception, values survival. In a film made of an actual abortion, the fetus could be seen on the sonar screen actually trying to get away from the abortionist's instrument. To a fetus life is a value. In other words, the value of survival is imprinted in the genetic code of each human being.

When an educator claims to be value-neutral, you can be sure that he is not talking about economics. He is referring to moral values. The term "moral values" is a marvelous invention by humanists calculated to undermine the idea of absolute morality. By simply using the term, one accepts the notion of competing, but equally valid, moral codes. That's how you get a society to accept the unacceptable — by inventing a phrase that, when used in discourse, tacitly implies acceptance. The idea that several moral codes can coexist in one society is then touted as the essence of democracy — freedom of choice, freedom to kill the unborn, freedom not to kill the unborn.

It is obvious that competing moral codes cannot coexist in a society without causing moral chaos. For example, the Biblical moral code, which was the morality of our Founding Fathers, the moral code on which our institutions were built, regards premarital sex as immoral. That didn't stop clandestine premarital affairs from occurring. But unwed motherhood was considered a cause for shame and was generally kept secret. The purpose of that moral code was to protect the integrity of marriage and the family, to protect women from the consequences of such behavior, to instill in young men a sense of responsibility in their romantic relationships, and to maintain a stable and healthy social order through marital fidelity and monogamy.

In this regard, the Biblical moral code calls for a healthy and logical course of behavior based on the natural order of things. Boy first meets girl. Boy and girl then get to know one another. Boy and girl then fall in love. Their families then meet each other. Boy and girl get engaged. Boy and girl get married. Boy and girl, now man and wife, go on honeymoon, move in together, and have a family. The result is marital happiness (which is not as uncommon as we've been led to believe), social stability, economic productivity, and children raised in an atmosphere of emotional security and loving relationships.

The alternative humanist moral code produces an entirely different scenario. That moral code is clearly spelled out in *Humanist Manifesto II* as follows:

> In the area of sexuality, we believe that intolerant attitudes, often cultivated by orthodox religions and puritanical cultures, unduly repress sexual conduct. The right to birth control,

abortion, and divorce should be recognized. While we do not approve of exploitive, denigrating forms of sexual expression, neither do we wish to prohibit, by law or social sanction, sexual behavior between consenting adults. The many varieties of sexual exploration should not in themselves be considered "evil." Without countenancing mindless permissiveness or unbridled promiscuity, a civilized society should be a tolerant one. Short of harming others or compelling them to do likewise, individuals should be permitted to express their sexual proclivities and pursue their lifestyles as they desire. We wish to cultivate the development of a responsible attitude toward sexuality, in which humans are not exploited as sexual objects, and in which intimacy, sensitivity, respect, and honesty in interpersonal relations are encouraged. Moral education for children and adults is an important way of developing awareness and sexual maturity.

What kind of behavior flows from the sexual recipe in this Manifesto? Here's a scenario we've seen enacted time and time again. Boy meets girl. Boy and girl have sex. Girl gets pregnant. Her pregnancy causes a family crisis. She's not sure what to do. Boy leaves girl. Girl decides on an abortion. The trauma of the abortion remains with her forever. She picks up the emotional pieces of her life and looks for another boyfriend.

Here's another scenario. Boy meets girl. Boy gets condom from guidance counselor in school clinic. Condom fails. Girl gets pregnant. Girl decides to have the child, live on welfare, and raise the child without a father. She and her child will live in a state of near-poverty until she finds someone who might marry her.

Here's a more middle-class scenario. Boy meets girl. Girl enters into a "meaningful relationship" with her boyfriend. They live together. She gets pregnant and proposes they get married. But boy convinces her they are not ready for marriage and that an abortion is the best solution. Girl has the abortion, becomes depressed, withholds sex from her boyfriend. Boy leaves girl for another "meaningful relationship" with the girl's best friend. Girl tries to commit suicide but botches the job. Modern middle-class mother hands her daughter a diaphragm for her birthday.

We could spend the rest of the day concocting an endless variety of scenarios — all ending up in one sort of tragedy or another. The humanists would contend that some of these premarital affairs actually end up in happy marriages.

But what has acceptance of and tolerance for premarital sex given us? Widespread unwed motherhood, an epidemic of venereal diseases seriously affecting the health of millions of young people, the massive killing of the unborn, increased unhappiness and depression caused by failed romances, abandonment by lovers, infidelity, and empty, degrading sexual affairs. That's the legacy of the new sexual morality. Not exactly a recipe for human happiness.

Clearly, what we have in America is a cultural civil war being fought not by armed regiments but by adherents of competing moral codes. This civil war has created not only moral chaos but judicial chaos. A moral code is enforced either by custom or by law, and a system of law that tries to reconcile such contradictory and irreconcilable moral customs and standards is doomed to fail.

The confusion that besets society is particularly acute when dealing with such volatile subjects as homosexuality and deviant lifestyles. The Biblical moral code, to which most Americans adhere, explicitly regards homosexuality not only as immoral but as an abomination — a rather strong, visceral condemnation if there ever was one. But society's disapproval never stopped homosexuality from existing. It was practiced secretly, out of public sight. But with the growing acceptance of the "new morality" among swinging heterosexuals in the 1960s, homosexuals began to assert their right to live their lifestyle openly and flagrantly. And the public generally acquiesced in the name of tolerance — that indispensable ingredient of a democratic society. The idea of religious tolerance was simply extended to cover sexual tolerance.

The result was a tremendous increase in promiscuous behavior among homosexuals. This increased enormously the spread of venereal diseases among them, culminating in the germination and spread of the deadly AIDS virus, which as of February 1991 has resulted in the deaths of over 100,000 individuals, 80 percent of them homosexuals. The Humanist Manifesto preaches sexual tolerance and the freedom of consenting adults to engage in any sexual activities they wish. The assumption is that if the activities are conducted among consenting adults, no harm can possibly come to anyone else. If only this were true!

The AIDS epidemic has demonstrated how easily a blood bank can transport the infected blood of a promiscuous homosexual in Los Angeles to the veins of a hospital patient undergoing surgery in Denver. It has demonstrated how easy it is for a pregnant intravenous drug user, infected by a contaminated needle, to pass the AIDS virus to her unborn child.

In other words, when a nation, in its magnanimity, tolerates perverse behavior, it pays a price it may not have anticipated. The humanists give the impression that the Biblical moral code is unduly repressive and intolerant for totally arbitrary, unjustifiable reasons. It is assumed that the Puritans disliked sex and all other forms of carnality because they were cold-blooded, coldhearted stick-in-the-muds, paralyzed by superstition and the fear of a monstrous, angry mythical figure called Jehovah.

But when one examines the Biblical moral code objectively, one finds in it the most reasonable, logical guide to a healthy, happy life one is likely to find anywhere. Clearly it is a moral code based on a profound understanding of human nature and human experience. It is unlikely, for example, that the AIDS plague is something new. Such plagues probably existed in ancient times among pagans whose sexual practices were similar to those practiced today by the adherents of the "new morality." Two thousand years of sexual self-control based on the tenets of the Ten Commandments simply eradicated most of these plagues. But now they are back — because the old practices are back.

Where did this destructive new morality come from? It came from a profoundly atheistic intellectual elite who adopted Freud's dictum that sexual repression is bad for your health. In 1933 the Humanist Manifesto championed for all Americans the sort of moral freedom that artists and writers in Greenwich Village had long enjoyed as one of the benefits of bohemian life. It took Hugh Hefner, with his newly launched *Playboy* magazine, to bring that hedonist philosophy to the business executive and university student. Artists and writers were no longer the privileged class. Middle-class America was now told that the forbidden fruit was now available to just about everyone at popular prices.

But something else had been going on at a deeper level to prepare America for its transformation into Sodom and Gomorrah. The battering ram against Biblical morality was not only the Humanist Manifesto, but the new humanistic psychology — otherwise known as the Third Force.

This new psychology was principally the work of a brilliant young psychologist named Abraham Maslow, who, working with the best of intentions and highest of moral aims, brought into being the human potential movement, which has led millions of Americans into moral and spiritual chaos.

Maslow, born in New York of a Jewish immigrant family in 1908, rejected religion early in life because he associated it with a mother he detested. He wrote in later years:

> I always wondered where my utopianism, ethical stress, humanism, stress on kindness, love, friendship, and all the rest came from. I knew certainly of the direct consequences of having no mother-love. But the whole thrust of my life-philosophy and all my research and theorizing also has its roots in a hatred for and revulsion against everything she stood for.

By the time Maslow was a teenager he regarded all religion as nonsensical. To him, religious observance attracted only the naive and hypocritical. Later, in high school, a teacher introduced him to the novels of Upton Sinclair, which turned him into a socialist. Eugene Debs, Norman Thomas, and other prominent American socialists became his heroes.

In 1928 Maslow chose psychology as his career after reading several essays by John B. Watson, the father of American behaviorism. "I suddenly saw unrolling before me into the future," he wrote, "the possibility of a science of psychology, a program of work which promised real progress, real advance, real solutions of real problems. All that was necessary was devotion and hard work."

Watson's anti-religious outlook strongly appealed to Maslow, who shared Watson's faith in rationality as the means to a better society. He was particularly taken in by Watson's optimistic belief in the malleability of human nature. Change the environment and you can change human nature, argued Watson.

However, it was through his field work with the Blackfoot Indians in Montana in the 1930s that Maslow began to revise his behaviorist views. He wrote: "It would seem that every human being comes at birth into society not as a lump of clay to be molded by society, but rather as a structure which society may warp or suppress or build upon. I am now struggling with a notion of a 'fundamental' or 'natural' personality structure."

But it was the birth of his daughter in 1938 that made Maslow reject behaviorism altogether. As he watched his little daughter assert her wants and dislikes, the idea that a child could be molded into anything the psychologist wanted through behavioral conditioning became untenable. He wrote: "Becoming a father changed my whole life.... It made the behaviorism I had been so enthusiastic about look so foolish that I couldn't stomach it anymore."

In 1943, Maslow formulated his own theory of human motivation. He centered his theory on what he called the hierarchy of human needs. He contended that every person is born with a set of basic needs, such as food, safety, love, self-esteem. But when these basic needs are satisfied, there is a higher need that cries for satisfaction: self-actualization.

He wrote: "A musician must make music, an artist must paint, a poet must write, if he is to be ultimately at peace with himself. What a man can be, he must be. This need we may call self-actualization."

Maslow had rejected Freud's pessimistic view of human nature and the behaviorists' animalistic view of man. He had come up with a third view of his own. He was much more interested in human success than in human failure. Maslow's biographer, Edward Hoffman, wrote:

> The issue was no longer "What makes for a genius like Beethoven?" but "Why aren't we all Beethovens?" Slowly and unexpectedly, Maslow's self-actualization research had become the basis for an entirely new vision of psychology with the

premise that each of us harbors an innate human nature of vast potential that usually becomes blocked or thwarted through the deprivation of lower needs. This inner potential, Maslow believed, had not been taken into account by any existing school of psychology…. (p. 173)

He emphasized that true fulfillment in life comes from satisfying our higher needs, especially the need for self-actualization. The more we pursue and realize our loftier needs, Maslow contended, the happier and even physically healthier we will be. (p.181)

Maslow himself wrote: "I think of the self-actualizing man not as an ordinary man with something added, but rather as an ordinary man with nothing taken away. The average man is a human being with dampened and inhibited powers." (p.174)

In short, Maslow had come up with another secular recipe for human perfectibility, in complete contradiction to the Biblical view of man's fallen nature. It is said that Maslow had a Messiah complex with a great personal mission to change the human condition. He said in 1955:

I am also very definitely interested and concerned with man's fate, with his ends and goals and with his future. I would like to help improve him and to better his prospects. I hope to help teach him how to be brotherly, cooperative, peaceful, courageous, and just. I think science is the best hope for achieving this, and of all the sciences, I consider psychology most important to this end. Indeed, I sometimes think that the world will either be saved by psychologists — in the very broadest sense — or else it will not be saved at all.

In other words, humanistic psychology offered mankind a new, atheistic road to salvation, and one of the mechanisms or techniques that the psychologists — or humanistic clergy — would use to bring salvation to the individual is the encounter group — the intensive group experience.

The encounter experience was first developed at the National Training Laboratory (NTL) in Bethel, Maine, sponsored by the National Education Association. It was founded in 1947 by Kurt Lewin, a German social psychologist who invented "sensitivity training" and "group dynamics," or the psychology of the collective. Lewin's work was very much in harmony with John Dewey's educational philosophy, which stressed socialization.

The man most responsible for joining the encounter movement with humanistic psychology was Carl Rogers, the founder of nondirective psychological counseling. In nondirective counseling, or teaching, the therapist, or teacher, is merely a facilitator who helps the client or pupil get in touch with his own feelings so that he can direct his own decision-making in accordance with his own values. In teaching, this encourages moral subjectivism and pupil rejection of all outside authority.

Rogers became the guru of the encounter movement because of his extensive experimentation with the technique at the Western Behavioral Sciences Institute (WBSI) at La Jolla, California. In a lecture to an audience of educators in 1968, Rogers described the function of the encounter group:

> One of the most effective means yet discovered for facilitating constructive learning, and growth, and change in individuals and in the organization they represent is the intensive group experience. It goes by many names: encounter group, T-group, sensitivity training....

> The intensive group or encounter group usually consists of ten to fifteen persons and a facilitator or leader. Personally, I like the term facilitator better because I think he really helps to facilitate the group in its own direction. It's a relatively unstructured group providing a climate of maximum freedom for personal expression, exploration of feelings and interpersonal communication.

The first sensitivity training program for educational leaders was conducted by the National Training Laboratory in 1959. It was cosponsored by the National Association of Elementary School Principals. The program was designed for the principal as an agent and manager of change. Rogers wrote:

Changingness, a reliance on process rather than upon static knowledge, is the only thing that makes any sense as a goal for education in the modern world.

Why all the emphasis on change? Because the humanists realized that there was something terribly wrong with public education and that it had to be changed. Rogers wrote in 1971:

> I have days when I think educational institutions at all levels are doomed. I also have moments when it seems that if we could only do away with state-required curricula, compulsory attendance, tenured professors, hours of lectures, grades, degrees, and all that, perhaps everybody could move outside the stifling hallowed walls and learning could flourish on its own.

But Rogers' dream was only a dream. Schools were here to stay, and the humanists were determined to remake them in their own image. Arthur Combs wrote:

> There are hundreds of ways we dehumanize people in our schools, and we need to make a systematic attempt to get rid of them.... If we want to humanize the processes of learning, we must make a systematic search for the things that destroy effective learning and remove them from the scene. If we're going to humanize the processes of learning, we must take the student in as a partner. Education wouldn't be irrelevant if students had a voice in decision making.

One must admit that the humanist critique had merit. Public education was every bit as bad as they said it was. But would sensitivity training, values clarification, and encounter groups make it better or worse? In 1971, John R. Silber, who later became president of Boston University wrote:

> Encounter groups invade human privacy with reckless abandon. You cannot make public what is private without changing it. We have derived our sense of human dignity largely from the Judeo-Christian tradition and, to some extent, from the Hellenic tradition. In rejecting those traditions, we forfeit the basis for the respect of the individual person and his dignity.

> I question the claim that encounter sessions have therapeutic value.... Some group sessions have caused great harm, bringing people over the brink., exacerbating mental difficulties and problems that were relatively under control before the students participated in encounter sessions.

What Silber suggested is that the encounter group was the humanists' equivalent of the prayer meeting. And there is no doubt that what Maslow and Rogers were offering America was a new religion in which self-actualization replaced salvation as the ultimate meaning and goal of life.

But how does all of this work in the classroom today? Humanistic psychology has been so widely accepted, so deeply absorbed and institutionalized by the education system, that the educators themselves see it as the system's underlying philosophy.

And that is why affective education is considered the indispensable part of the public school curriculum. Why? Because it deals with values, beliefs, feelings, and behavior. As Arthur Combs said:

> Modern education must produce far more than persons with cognitive skills. It must produce humane individuals.... We can live with a bad reader; a bigot is a danger to everyone.

> What is needed is a humanistic psychology expressly designed to deal with the human aspects of personality and behavior, a psychology which does not ignore the students' belief systems but makes them central to its concerns.

When I was going to elementary school back in the 1930s, the last thing the teacher was concerned with were my feelings or belief system. She didn't want to know how or what I felt. She wanted to know if I was learning what she was teaching.

Affective education has opened the schoolhouse door to every sort of lunacy the humanists can dream up. We not only have sex education, sensitivity training, and values clarification, but also death education, drug education, magic circles, role playing, transcendental meditation, yoga, Eastern religion, etc.

One widely used technique for clarifying values in the classroom is the lifeboat survival game, or fallout shelter game. I was given the instruction sheet for the latter exercise by a parent in Clarkston, Washington, where I was lecturing. It was used in the ninth grade at the local high school. Ninth graders are about fourteen or fifteen years old.

The lesson is entitled, "Who Should Survive," and the instructions read:

> The following fifteen persons are in a bomb shelter after a nuclear war. These fifteen persons are the only humans left on the earth. It will take six weeks for the external radiation level to drop to a safe survival level. The food and supplies in the shelter can sustain at a very minimum level, seven persons for six weeks. It is your task to decide which seven persons will survive. Be prepared to justify your choices.

First of all, notice how the problem is rigged. How do these fifteen persons know that they are the only humans left on earth? How do they know that it will take six weeks for the outside radiation level to fall? If they have that kind of scientific knowledge, maybe they also have a radiation-proof suit that one of the survivors can put on and find adequate food somewhere on the outside. Also, who among the survivors has the right to decide who is to live and who is to die? None of these questions are brought up. Instead, these fifteen-year-olds are now supposed to play God and sentence eight people to death in a situation that could easily be changed with a little imagination and resourcefulness.

Here are the fifteen persons:

1. Dr. Dame, 39, white, no church affiliation, Ph.D. in history, college professor, good health, married, one child, active, and enjoys politics.

2. Mrs. Dame, 38, white, Jew, M.A. in psychology, counselor in mental health clinic, good health, married, one child, active in community.

3. Bobby Dame, 10, white, Jew, special education classes for four years, mentally retarded, IQ 70, good health, enjoys his pets.

4. Mrs. Garcia, 33, Spanish-American, Roman Catholic, one child three weeks old, ninth grade education, cocktail waitress, prostitute, good health, abandoned as a child, in a foster home as a youth, attacked by foster father at age twelve, ran away from home, returned to reformatory, stayed until sixteen, married at sixteen, divorced at eighteen.

5. Jean Garcia, three weeks old, Spanish-American, good health, nursing for food.

6. Mrs. Evans, 32, Negro, Protestant, A.B. and M.A. in elementary education, teacher, divorced, one child, good health, cited as outstanding teacher, enjoys working with children.

7. Mary Evans, 8, Negro, Protestant, third grade, good health, excellent student.

8. John Jacobs, 13, white, Protestant, eighth grade, honor student, very active, broad interests, father is a Baptist minister, good health.

9. Mr. Newton, 25, Negro, claims to be an atheist, was in last year of medical school until suspended for homosexual activity, good health, seems bitter concerning racial problems, wears hippy clothes.

10. Mrs. Clark, 28, Negro, Protestant, college grad, engineering, electronics engineer, married, no children, good health, enjoys outdoor sports and stereo equipment, grew up in ghetto.

11. Sister Mary Kathleen, 27, nun, college grad, English major, grew up in upper-middle-class neighborhood, good health, father a businessman.

12. Mr. Blake, 51, white, Mormon, HS grad, mechanic, "Mr. Fix-it," married, four children (not with him), good health, enjoys outdoors and working in his shop.

13. Miss Harris, 21, Spanish-American, Protestant, college senior, nursing major, good health, enjoys outdoor sports, likes people.

14. Father Franz, 37, white, Catholic, college plus seminary, priest, active in civil rights, criticized for liberal views, good health, former college athlete.

15. Dr. Gonzales, 66, Spanish-American, Catholic, medical doctor,

general practitioner, has had two heart attacks in the past five years but continues to practice.

That completes our cast of characters. And now we can start clarifying our values. I can imagine the students deciding to get rid of the easy ones first — Bobby Dame, the mentally retarded Jewish boy, and Dr. Gonzales who will probably have his third heart attack before the six weeks are up. It's interesting to note that in Hitler's Germany, Nazi doctors decided that the mentally defective were socially worthless and should therefore be killed. This practice started in the 1930s, before the war.

Two more easy victims are Mrs. Garcia, the ex-prostitute, and her nursing infant. The fifth will no doubt be the black homosexual atheist who wears hippy clothes. He's hardly the type you'd want to help generate a new human race. So far it's been pretty easy. But we have three more to go.

Dr. and Mrs. Dame look pretty safe. He's got a Ph.D. and she's got an M.A., which means they can start a graduate school of psychology as soon as they crawl out of the shelter. Goodness knows the seven survivors will need one to help create their new world order. Mrs. Evans, the thirty-two-year-old black teacher, and her eight-year-old daughter look safe. Mrs. Evans has an A.B. and an M.A. in elementary education, which means that the education establishment will have survived the nuclear holocaust. John Jacobs, the thirteen-year-old white boy is a shoo-in. The kids in the class will certainly identify with him.

Mrs. Clark, the twenty-eight-year-old black electronics engineer, will probably be spared because she's good at repairing stereo equipment. Sister Mary Kathleen, the twenty-seven-year-old nun, is obviously a loser, unless she's willing to give up her virginity. Mr. Blake, the Mormon mechanic, is a little too old, all of fifty-one. Besides, he doesn't have a college degree. Miss Harris, the twenty-one-year-old Hispanic nursing major, looks good as a future breeder of children. Father Franz, the thirty-seven-year-old priest, is a problem. Maybe the kids will permit him to live if he gives up his celibacy.

Tough decisions for the kids to make. And, of course, this exercise has afforded the children the opportunity to discuss such subjects as infanticide, mercy killing, euthanasia, homosexuality, rape, prostitution, interracial marriage, religion, ethnic differences, etc. Incidentally, this cast of characters tells us much about the values of the educator who dreamed it up. If you will notice, five of the fifteen persons are white males; the one black male is a homosexual, and the one Hispanic male is old and sick. So only white males will survive. Of the five white males, the Ph.D., the thirteen-year-old boy and either the Mormon mechanic or the priest will be among the final winners. Did you ever doubt that the Ph.D. would survive?

As for the females, the situation is fraught with social and racial overtones. The exercise starts with eight females: two whites (the Master of Psychology and the nun); three blacks (the M.A. in elementary education, her daughter, and the electronics engineer); and three Hispanics (the prostitute and her baby and the student nurse). After eliminating the prostitute and her baby, the kids will have to eliminate two more. Who will they be? The nun? One or both of the strong black females? The Hispanic student nurse or the Master of Psychology? Maybe Dr. Dame will take a shine to one of the black females and decide that Mrs. Dame, the lone surviving Jew, is dispensable. Who needs a Jewish problem in the brave new world? Or maybe the Mormon mechanic and the thirteen-year-old boy will decide to solve the race problem once and for all by eliminating the three black females. Why start off a new world and a new human race with a race problem? The possibilities are positively enticing.

Well, have your values been sufficiently clarified? Can you imagine the emotional turmoil and confusion such an exercise can cause in the minds and hearts of the fifteen-year-olds who are forced to deal with it? The exercise clarifies nothing. It's a kind of moral masturbation that humanists love to engage in. It confuses the whole issue of values. Above all, it tells you that there is something sick in an educational system that conducts education in this perverse, depressing, idiotic way.

Incidentally, when I was given this class exercise by the parent in Clarkston and read it, I complained about it in a press interview. I thought it was pretty awful. The principal of the high school was informed of my complaint. He defended the assignment as one that teaches students the "process one goes about in making choices." He said that the exercise was not unrealistic in this age of nuclear issues and that not to discuss such issues would be a disservice to the students.

Think about that for a moment. The principal would have us believe that it is perfectly realistic for children to think of themselves as one of fifteen sole survivors in a worldwide nuclear holocaust. Statistically, it is far more likely that any one of these children will win the state lottery or the Irish Sweepstakes than find himself among the last fifteen survivors of the human race. So why not give the children an exercise in deciding what they would do with fifteen million dollars if they won it in a lottery? It would be a lot more fun, a lot more realistic (for hundreds of people in America have actually faced that problem), and a lot healthier than ordering the executions of eight survivors of a nuclear holocaust. One would think that in such a situation, every human being would be precious enough to want to save. But humanists don't think that way.

I believe that what makes humanism and humanistic psychology so malevolent, so destructive, is their profound atheism, an atheism not based on indifference toward God, but hatred and defiance. It is not insignificant that what drove Maslow in search of the secular holy grail was the hatred he had for his mother and everything he thought she represented. He never forgave her. He even refused to attend her funeral. Yet toward the end of his life he could see that he had made some serious mistakes in his psychological scheme. But by then his ideas had been absorbed by so many hedonists and pagans and lunatics that the damage could never be undone.

And so the civil war continues. How it will end no one knows. However, there is a faint silver lining off in the distance. The home-school movement, which grows stronger by the day, indicates that many families in America are willing to take matters into their own hands when it comes to the education of their own children.

Their abandonment of the public school represents a radical break with the cultural and statist norms of our society. Something fundamental is taking place when citizens abandon institutions that were once considered sacred.

The only solution to this conflict over values is to restore full educational freedom in America, to get the government out of the education business, thereby diminishing the political and economic power of the education establishment, and to repeal the compulsory attendance laws that make our youngsters virtual prisoners of the state for twelve years. When people argue that without compulsory attendance some children will not go to school, I reply that no school is better than public school.

I feel sad in having to say this because I went to public schools and got a fairly decent education. But that was half a century ago. Things are different today, and we must move forward. Frankly, I am convinced that public education is doomed. It is a sick dinosaur destined for extinction. It no longer works, and it survives only because of its political power.

What value is there in a system that doesn't work and can't work? Recently, John Gatto, who was named New York City's Teacher of the Year, appeared before a hearing in which he castigated the school system for "the murder of one million black and Latino children." He got a standing ovation.

This country has indeed reached a point of decision, but the decision isn't being made by the educators or our political leaders. It is being made every day by parents who now know that there is no other way to change things. And that's the way it will probably be for some years to come.

THE IMPORTANCE OF HOMESCHOOLING TO AMERICA

We are just beginning to understand how profoundly significant the homeschool movement has become, particularly at this time in our history when we are engaged in a full-fledged cultural war between humanism and Christianity, when government officials can behave in ways totally contrary to what our Constitution tells us is permissible.

For example, when federal agents are used to invade a home and seize a child at gunpoint and take him to his communist father who wants to take him back to communist Cuba, we must ask ourselves, is that the proper way to solve a custody case? Custody battles are supposed to be settled by courts, not by SWAT teams. But poor, misguided Janet Reno, who was responsible for the attack at Waco that ended with the incineration of eighty or so men, women, and children, doesn't seem to have learned much from her earlier blunder.

The excuse used in both the Waco and Elian cases was that it was necessary to save the children from abuse. They used charlatan psychologists to bolster the case for child abuse without even having interviewed the children. Does anyone have any doubt that there are psychiatrists in America who would be more than willing to testify that a homeschooled child is being abused by his parents because he is being denied socialization in a public school?

Many educators consider homeschoolers to be fanatics. For example, one such educator, a professor by the name of David Blacker, wrote in the February 1998 issue of the *American Journal of Education* an article entitled "Fanaticism and Schooling in the Democratic State," in which he said:

> In both its spectacular terroristic forms and, perhaps even more so, in its quieter and currently expanding institutional

agendas, what I shall call "fanaticism" challenges the democratic constituted state to its core. Nowhere is this challenge
more acute than in the educational arena in which tectonic
shiftings in the century-old United States public school movement have given rise to a range of particularist initiatives —
charter schools, vouchers, "parents' rights," a variety of ethno-
centricism, home schooling as a national movement — which
provide cover and legitimization for an array of emboldened
fanatical groups. ...Schools run by fanatics, as I shall argue, act
so severely against these democratic premises that, whatever
else we decide we want to do or want to try, we must not permit them in any form....

Obviously, Professor Blacker is hardly a friend of educational freedom. Do you want to know how he defines a fanatic? He wrote:
"A fanatic...must possess beliefs that are characterized by both their
single-mindedness and comprehensiveness."

Christians, of course, are known for their single-minded belief
in God, their single-minded adherence to the gospel of Jesus Christ,
and their comprehensive Biblical worldview that radically differs
from the worldviews of secular humanists, atheists, communists, and
socialists.

We are indeed involved in a cultural civil war, the outcome of
which will determine whether or not America remains the land of
individual and religious freedom that we inherited from our forefathers, and whether or not we shall be able to pass on to future generations this precious legacy of freedom.

Totalitarians in America don't like what homeschoolers are doing because they have freed themselves from state education, they
have liberated themselves from the governmental institutions that
want to brainwash their children so that they will become willing
servants of the state.

Homeschoolers have become a bulwark against government
tyranny. That's the political reality that all homeschoolers must face.
And they must face it cheerfully, believing that most Americans truly
want what they want: well-educated, well-behaved children, created
in the image of God, with a love of God and country. Achieving edu-

cational freedom has not been easy, but with the help of the Home School Legal Defense Association, homeschoolers have been able to assert their parental rights to educate their children in accordance with their own beliefs and values.

As for academics, homeschoolers have proven through their experiences that they are better educators than the professionals in the government system. What an affront to those certified professionals! How can parents possibly be better educators than they are? But parents are better educators for one simple reason: they truly believe in education, while the professionals no longer do. They don't even know how to teach children to read, or write, or do arithmetic. In fact, their stated aim is to dumb down the nation so that they can impose their rule with little or no resistance.

Unbelievable? One high-ranking Harvard professor, Anthony D. Oettinger, chairman of the Harvard Program on Information Resources Policy and a member of the Council on Foreign Relations, said in 1982:

> Our idea of literacy, I am afraid, is obsolete because it rests on a frozen and classical definition....The present "traditional" concept of literacy has to do with the ability to read and write. But the real question that confronts us today is: How do we help citizens function well in their society? How can they acquire the skills necessary to solve their problems? Do we, for example, really want to teach people to do a lot of sums or write in "a fine round hand" when they have a five-dollar hand-held calculator or a word processor to work with? Or, do we really have to have everybody literate — writing and reading in the traditional sense — when we have the means in our technology to achieve a new flowering of oral communication? What is speech recognition and speech synthesis all about it if does not lead to ways of reducing the burden on the individual of the imposed notions of literacy that were a product of nineteenth century economics and technology?

I could write a book critiquing that Harvard professor's views on literacy. He doesn't like the traditional concept of literacy — which is really the one that homeschoolers adhere to. Homeschoolers want their children to become fluent readers. That's why they use phonics. He says children don't have to be taught arithmetic or writing because they've got little calculators and word processors. But how can a student use a word processor unless he is literate? Then he says: "Do we really have to have everybody literate?" What he means is that some people, an elite, have to be literate, but the rest of the population can be semi-literate and use oral communication, like music. In this new social order, who decides who is to become literate and who is not?

Professor Oettinger doesn't want to impose on American children notions of literacy that were a product of nineteenth-century economics and technology. What he chooses to forget is that literacy was high in early America because of the need to be able to read the Bible and know the Word of God. To our forefathers the purpose of education was to pass on to the next generation the knowledge, wisdom, and values of the previous generation. To our forefathers, man was made in God's image and therefore children had to be educated with that concept in mind. And for Christian homeschoolers that is also the purpose of education.

I don't know of any parent who sends a child to school not to learn to read, write, and do arithmetic. But the top professionals are telling us that these are things not all children have to learn. So why do we have compulsory school attendance? So that they can keep asking for billions of more dollars for education. What kind of education are they talking about? They're talking about values clarification, multiculturalism, sex education, death education, drug education, sensitivity training, evolution, and a whole lot of other programs that have nothing to do with learning basic academic skills. That's what all of that money is being used for.

And that's why homeschoolers have left the government system. The government schools no longer educate. Their main activity is behavior modification through emotional manipulation, and they use psychotherapy to change a child's values and beliefs. It was Professor Benjamin Bloom, a behavioral scientist at the University of Chicago, who set the standards and guidelines for Outcome Based Education in a book entitled *Taxonomy of Educational Objectives*, published in 1956 and 1964. He wrote:

> This taxonomy is designed to be a classification of the student behaviors which represent the intended outcomes of the educational process....What we are classifying is the intended behavior of students — the ways in which individuals are to act, think, or feel as the result of participating in some unit of instruction.

When I was going to public school in the 1930s, the last thing my teachers were interested in were my feelings. They didn't want to know how I felt about reading, writing, or arithmetic. They wanted to know if I was learning what they were teaching, and that was easily done by periodic tests. There were no complex national tests in those days to see if a student could read and write. The classroom teacher knew whether or not her students could read or write; she made sure that they could because she knew how to teach reading and writing. This is not always true of today's teachers, many of whom are themselves semiliterate. Professor Bloom, commenting on the difficulties involved in changing values, made this significant statement:

> The evidence points out convincingly to the fact that age is a factor operating against attempts to effect a complete or thoroughgoing reorganization of attitudes and values....The evidence collected thus far suggests that a single hour of classroom activity under certain conditions may bring about a major reorganization in cognitive as well as affective behaviors.

Educators now consider it their primary task to effect a complete or thoroughgoing reorganization of attitudes and values. They're out to take our children and rid them of the values and morals that we have taught them. They're out to destroy family harmony and replace it with family conflict. This is not what the education system of a free people should be doing. But we can't stop them from doing it because they have the support of state and national legislators. They have access to billions of taxpayer dollars.

Put simply but accurately, American public education has become a human-animal management system. Its purpose is to control the minds and movements of forty million young Americans, using compulsory school attendance laws to force these millions of children into government buildings where their time can be managed and their access to real education restricted. Mind and behavioral control is the true purpose of the system, which is now called the Human Resources Development System. And all of this is being willingly paid for by the taxpayer who has been deluded into thinking that something of true value goes on in those public schools. The public school has become more like a concentration camp than an institution for learning. Psychotherapy is the method used to deprogram the children from their family's values and reprogram them into compliant animals. They are trained to become mere processors of information, with empty heads and empty souls.

And that is why the homeschooling movement has assumed an importance that cannot be overestimated. Homeschool educators are good at teaching American history, which is essential if we are to defend our heritage. The Declaration of Independence, our founding document, was written by and for men created in the image of God. It is so vitally important because it defines what government is all about.

> We hold these truths to be self-evident, that all men are created equal; that they are endowed by their Creator with certain unalienable rights; that among these, are life, liberty, and the pursuit of happiness. That, to secure these rights, governments are instituted among men, deriving their just powers from the consent of the governed.

This is very simple, direct language, easy to understand. The purpose of government is to secure the unalienable rights of the people, rights endowed by God, not handed down by government. Homeschoolers are exercising their God-given, unalienable right to educate their children in accordance with their own values and religious beliefs.

The United States Constitution is based on the principles outlined in the Declaration. That's why it remains our ultimate protection against political tyranny. We have a Second Amendment, the right of citizens to own and bear arms, that gives teeth to the Constitution. Without that Second Amendment, the Constitution would just be a piece of paper that politicians could rip up at will.

It is the homeschool movement that permits me to be optimistic about the American future. More and more parents are discovering the value of educational freedom, and more and more Americans are becoming aware of the true nature of what public education has become. It takes a Columbine to wake some of them up. But even with a Columbine, most parents will still put their children in a school that reeks of satanic influences.

The homeschool movement has grown mightily in the last decade. In my state of Massachusetts, we have a state organization that began having conventions ten years ago. There were about 300 people at that first convention held in a church basement. Ten years later, there wasn't a hotel large enough to accommodate the convention that attracted over 3,000. They had to rent the convention center in Worcester, the state's second largest city.

This is the kind of growth we see all over the country. We are slowly, quietly, and steadily taking back our country. Homeschoolers are now getting into politics and running for office. Michael Farris, President of the Home School Legal Defense Association, has founded Patrick Henry College to educate homeschoolers to work in Congress. Homeschooled graduates are entering every profession and pursuing all sorts of careers. Because they are literate and know more than the average public schooler, they will have advantages in the working world. Home educators are very important to America. They are the purveyors of God's curriculum to their children who will thus be well prepared to enter the battle to preserve our constitutional republic. It has required tremendous effort and dedication to have created a movement so vibrant, so strong in its convictions, so devoted to the moral and intellectual development of future generations. There is no doubt in my mind that the great Founding Fathers of this country would be enormously pleased to see that homeschoolers are upholding what they fought and died for. The price of our freedom has been the blood of our forefathers. American soldiers have fought and died for the very ideals that homeschoolers are upholding on the home front.

The enemy in this war is within our gates. That's where the battles will be fought: in courts, state legislatures, Congress, in the universities, in the arts, in the media. But education will decide where the future generations take us. I won't be around to see it. But I know that the spirit of liberty, which is so strong among homeschoolers, will prevail in the end. May God bless the homeschool in all that it does to raise a new generation of patriots — well grounded in the Bible, the Declaration of Independence, and the Constitution of the United States.

WHAT THE HOMESCHOOL MOVEMENT SHOULD BE DOING IN THE NEW MILLENNIUM

What should the Christian homeschool movement be doing in the new millennium? First and foremost, it should be reaffirming God's curriculum. If we want to understand what that curriculum is, all we have to do is read Genesis 1:26-28:

> And God said, Let us make man in our image, after our likeness: and let them have dominion over the fish of the sea, and over the fowl of the air, and over the cattle, and over all the earth, and over every creeping thing that creepeth upon the earth. So God created man in his own image, in the image of God created he him; male and female created he them. And God blessed them, and God said unto them, Be fruitful and multiply, and replenish the earth, and subdue it.

What does this mean? It means that God created man to be like Him, not to be another god, but to be like God, with creative powers and intelligence that no other creature possessed. The ability to have dominion meant that man would be superior to the animal kingdom, be separate and apart from it, and be able to make use of it for his benefit. To replenish the earth and subdue it meant that man was to become a farmer, a horticulturist, a gardener, a true conservationist. He was to treat the earth as his possession, a gift, to be nurtured, cared for, and from which he could gain nourishment and wealth. God also gave man the power of language, which was not given to any animal. It was the power of language — the power of definition — that permitted man to take dominion and convert God's raw materials into food, clothing, and shelter.

God then did something quite significant. We read in Genesis 2:19-20:

> And out of the ground the LORD God formed every beast of the field and every fowl of the air, and brought them unto Adam to see what he would call them: and whatsoever Adam called every living creature, that was the name thereof. And Adam gave names to all cattle, and to the fowl of the air, and to every beast of the field.

In other words, God made Adam into an observer of the natural world, a scientist, and a lexicographer — an expander of language, a maker of dictionaries. This was God's first step in educating Adam, to make sure that Adam knew he was not an animal, that he was apart from the animal kingdom, with gifts that permitted him to dominate the animal world. In other words, man was created by God to be a scientist, explorer, inventor, and educator of his children.

God, in His creative and loving magnanimity, programmed man's brain with the innate faculty of language. That is why every child learns to speak his own language virtually from birth, so that by the time he is ready for some kind of formal education, he has developed a speaking vocabulary in the thousands of words. The gift of language was the necessary and indispensable instrument for dominion.

That, in sum, is God's curriculum, a curriculum profoundly in opposition to the humanist curriculum that now permeates American public education. There has been much talk about what happened at Columbine High School in Littleton, Colorado. The government believes that guns were the cause of the problem and, therefore, the confiscation of all guns in America is their logical solution.

But there is no doubt in my mind that the cause of the murders at Columbine is the satanic curriculum that still permeates that high school, a curriculum that embraces death education, sex education, multiculturalism, sensitivity training, transcendental meditation, values clarification, drug education, and, most importantly, evolution. Evolution teaches children that they are animals, that they were not made in the image of God but in the image of a monkey. Why, then, should we be surprised when children begin to act like animals?

What the Christian homeschool movement must do in the new millennium is exactly what it has been doing since the movement began: reaffirming Biblical religion and morality, maintaining its independence from government, building its strength, educating children with the knowledge that they were made in the image of God, promoting the idea of educational freedom, and producing the future leaders of America.

The Christian homeschool movement draws its strength, its purpose, its vision, from the Bible — from Deuteronomy — in which parents are commanded to educate their children in the knowledge and admonition of God. It is important to love God but also to fear Him. One of the reasons why so many youngsters today have no fear of authority is because they have no fear of God. Christian homeschoolers must transfer the basic precepts of Deuteronomy from one generation to the next. That is the only way that Biblical religion can influence the future. That is why the public schools work so hard to stymie and block that transfer. The humanists do not want Biblical religion to influence the future. They want Biblical religion to be relegated to the dead past, like the dinosaur.

To give you an idea of how deeply the humanists despise Biblical religion, let me quote an essay from *The Humanist* magazine of January 1983, written by a young humanist scholar by the name of John Dunphy:

> I am convinced that the battle for humankind's future must be waged and won in the public school classroom by teachers who correctly perceive their role as the proselytizers of a new faith: a religion of humanity that recognizes and respects the spark of what theologians call divinity in every human being.

> These teachers must embody the same selfless dedication as the most rabid fundamentalist preachers, for they will be ministers of another sort, utilizing a classroom instead of a pulpit to convey humanist values in whatever subject they teach, regardless of educational level — preschool day care or large state university. The classroom must and will become an arena of conflict between the old and the new — the rotting corpse of Christianity, together with its adjacent evils and misery, and

the new faith of humanism, resplendent in its promise of a world in which the never-realized Christian ideal of "love thy neighbor" will finally be achieved.

Mr. Dunphy won a prize for that essay. It represents humanist thinking as clearly and bluntly as anyone could state it. The humanists mean business. Read the two humanist manifestos to know their complete program. They talk of humankind's future, not just America's future, not just the future of their own children. They're talking about all children and their future. And they're doing a great job of converting lots of Christian children who attend public schools. The two killers at Columbine were converted from their family religions to satanism. There is hardly a Christian family in America that hasn't lost a child to humanism or satanism or nihilism.

But thank God, homeschoolers have removed their children from those proselytizers of the new faith in which there is no God, no sexual restraint, in which abortion is allowed and encouraged, morality is situational, and ethics are relative. Look at what is going on in today's public schools: the killings, the sexual promiscuity, the drug trafficking, and the suicides. That's what humanism is doing to American youth. The sad thing is that parents, many of whom go to church on Sunday, are letting it happen.

Need I say more about the importance of the Christian homeschool movement as a positive force for America's future in the new millennium? And that is all the more reason for homeschoolers to maintain their independence from government. As homeschoolers have discovered through their own experience, government is not needed in education. Homeschooling parents have proven that they can educate their children very well without government bureaucrats and certified teachers breathing down their necks. They have learned what the early founders of this country knew: that parents, for the most part, are the best educators of their own children.

Now, I must say that there was a time when the public schools did adhere to Biblical morality. For example, when I was in elementary school in New York City in the 1930s, the principal read the Twenty-third Psalm at the opening of each assembly. That reading had a profound effect on me. Most people know it by heart:

> The LORD is my shepherd; I shall not want. He maketh me to lie down in green pastures; he leadeth me beside the still waters. He restoreth my soul: he leadeth me in the paths of righteousness for his name's sake. Yea, though I walk through the valley of the shadow of death, I will fear no evil: for thou art with me; thy rod and thy staff they comfort me. Thou preparest a table before me in the presence of mine enemies: thou anointest my head with oil; my cup runneth over. Surely goodness and mercy shall follow me all the days of my life: and I will dwell in the house of the LORD for ever.

If children hear that psalm often enough, and repeat it to themselves, it will leave an indelible impression on their hearts and minds. But a principal in a public school can't read that psalm or any other psalm anymore. But homeschoolers can. That's the difference. That's the advantage children have over those trapped in the public schools. And that's why homeschooled, they can enter the new millennium with a tremendously optimistic view of the future. Their cups runneth over with the love and protection of God and the love and protection of their parents. They *will* walk down the paths of righteousness for His name's sake. How great America would be if *all* its children were led down that path!

The government schools have been taken over by the enemies of Christianity. They have been taken over by behavioral psychologists. And there's a good reason why Mr. Dunphy wants to start proselytizing the children in preschool day care. The late Benjamin Bloom, behaviorist professor at the University of Chicago, architect of today's public school curriculum known as Outcome Based Education, wrote:

> The evidence points out convincingly to the fact that age is a factor operating against attempts to effect a complete or thoroughgoing reorganization of attitudes and values....The evidence collected this far suggests that a single hour of classroom activity under certain conditions may bring about a major reorganization in cognitive as well as affective behaviors.

That is why so many parents, like those at Columbine High School, are at a loss to understand how their perfectly normal children can turn into killers or drug addicts or monstrous rebels. What they don't understand is that today's teachers are spending more time effecting a complete or thoroughgoing reorganization of their children's attitudes and values than teaching them the basic academic skills. Children are no longer students; they are patients undergoing psychotherapy. That's why they emerge from the schools with empty heads and high self-esteem, and hearts full of anger, frustration, and violence.

I make these points to strengthen the resolve of home educators to resist the pressure from those friends and relatives who think that what they are doing is wrong. Leaders in the Christian homeschool movement must also warn homeschoolers to beware of what the government schools will offer to get homeschooled children back: free computers and books. God's curriculum can only be provided by Christian parents.

It is important for the homeschool movement to maintain its independence, for without educational freedom, there will be no freedom for Christians or anybody else in America. Independence permits home educators to influence America in a Christian way through the education of children who will absorb their values and pass them on to their own children.

Also, by asserting the independence of the homeschool movement, home educators are affirming the fact that education is primarily a parental responsibility. God has given us four forms of government over which He maintains sovereignty: individual government, which must obey the Biblical restraints placed on individual behavior; family government, which must observe God's laws pertaining to family life, particularly the education of children; church government, which must exist under Biblical precepts; and civil government, which must exercise its powers in accordance with God's law. The civil government may not rule over church government or family government. Yet today civil bureaucrats have replaced God's sovereignty with government sovereignty.

The Christian homeschool movement must become a power that can fight the politicians and legislators who are beholden to the teachers' unions. That means becoming lobbyists in every state legislature and governing entity. In California, it means gaining clout in Sacramento. After all, homeschooling parents pay taxes and are voters, too.

Some years ago I advocated creating a Home Education Week in which homeschoolers would visit the governor and state legislature and give the representatives and senators a cherry pie, reminding them of George Washington's legacy and the fact that he was homeschooled. That week could also be used to educate the public as to the benefits derived from homeschoolers: lower taxes because homeschoolers pay for their own children's education; better behaved children; a safer community; and volunteer services, which homeschooled children can render the community.

Homeschoolers must also get involved in politics, because their freedom depends on what politicians do in the legislatures. There are by now some homeschooling dads already sitting in some state legislatures and even the Congress. We need many more of them. Back in the old days there were more farmers in the legislatures than lawyers. Now there are more public school educators in some legislatures than lawyers. It is time for homeschoolers to get into the act. Many of them would make wonderful legislators. Politics need not be a dirty business if practiced by believing Christians.

Homeschoolers should help those candidates who are sympathetic to homeschooling and educate those candidates who know little or nothing about the homeschool movement. Political activism should be part of every home educational program, because it teaches your children how the American government works, and how it can be manipulated by the enemies of Christianity and homeschooling.

Also, homeschoolers should use the new technology to improve the effectiveness of God's curriculum. High literacy and books, of course, come first. Language and literacy are the foundation of computer technology and the Internet. The more literate the person, the better able he will be to use a word processor, to use desktop publishing, and to create his own website. The Internet is proving to be a vital means of communication for homeschoolers. Today, I can download tons of information about the homeschool movement if I want to. It's amazing how much information is now available on the Web.

But don't let that detract a home educator from the task of raising a literate child for whom books, not the Internet, will be a joyful, intimate source of wisdom and literary pleasure. A child can curl up with a book whose author speaks to him directly and enters his consciousness and expands his mind. No one can curl up with a computer. The Internet provides information, not wisdom. Get children to love reading so that they will cherish books and build their own personal libraries.

The homeschool movement must also produce the leaders of tomorrow. I must give enormous credit to the intelligent vision of Michael Farris, president of the Home School Legal Defense Association, who has launched Patrick Henry College. I can't think of a better way to advance the cause of education and freedom in America than by establishing a college where homeschoolers can learn the ins and outs of our system of government and go directly to work, helping conservative congressmen do their jobs better and more effectively. I urge everyone to support Patrick Henry College in any way that is possible. I predict that in twenty years it will become a strong and vital university, a kind of academic West Point for homeschoolers seeking to return the American government to what it once was: a protector of freedom and not a wanton waster of the national treasure, turning the American people into vassals of bureaucratic overlords.

That, in a nutshell, should be the agenda of homeschoolers in the new millennium. We stand on the threshold of exciting times, where the call of freedom now seems to be echoing worldwide. Interest in homeschooling as an alternative to government-coerced brainwashing is spreading across the globe, thanks to what home educators are doing in America. I have long stopped looking to Washington, or Congress, or a political party to bring America back to its Biblical values. But when I see what Christian homeschoolers are doing, one family at a time, one child at time, to rebuild our Christian heritage, then I realize that that is where the revolution is taking place. The fact that homeschoolers have separated themselves from the humanist, statist institution of public education, and proven that they can do a better job than the so-called certified professionals, means that they are the true revolutionaries.

Homeschoolers have risen to the occasion, acting in much the same way that our Founding Fathers did when they signed the Declaration of Independence and set out to separate themselves from the tyranny of George III. Indeed, the Christian homeschool movement is entering the new millennium with strength and confidence and determination to do God's work in America.

COLUMBINE HIGH
AND NEW AGE PHILOSOPHY

One of the reasons why the educrats have focused on guns as the chief cause of the Littleton massacre is because Columbine High School was supposed to be the kind of progressive school where such things could never happen. Columbine High, built in 1973 and renovated in 1995 at a cost of 13.4 million dollars, was noted for its academic and athletic records. To many educators, it was a model of what an American high school should be. But perhaps we can better understand the moral permissiveness of the school if we review some recent history.

In 1990, the Mid-continent Regional Educational Laboratory (McREL), based in Denver, Colorado, received a 12.9 million dollar grant from the U.S. Deptartment of Education to help implement Outcome Based Education (OBE) in Colorado. The plan was called Direction 2000 and adopted at Littleton High School. In the Direction 2000 newsletter of June 1, 1990, Littleton High principal Tim Westerberg stated:

> Littleton High School is proposing a system of schooling which will be driven by a new set of 'outcome-based' graduation requirements, will provide a Program Advisor to work with each student during his or her stay at LHS, and will award diplomas to students who have demonstrated mastery of the 'outcome-based' graduation requirements through portfolios and exhibitions before a graduation committee. Balanced assessment and attention to each student's intellectual, social, physical, ethical, artistic, and emotional development are central to the project.

Although Columbine High School is not in the Littleton school district, it is hard to believe that it completely escaped the influences of the OBE-oriented school restructuring movement. The fact that

135

the two little Nazis, Harris and Klebold, were able freely to express themselves by dress and by a video advocating violence suggests that the school's educational philosophy is based on anything but Biblical principles.

If the school's operating philosophy did not come from Judeo-Christian principles, where did it come from? The answer is to be found in the New Age philosophy that was the moving spirit behind OBE. Carol Belt, a former school board member in Englewood, Colorado, was chairman of a Strategic Planning Committee in charge of drawing up "vision statements" about the future. She wrote: "As background material to help with the process I received materials on globalism and books by 'futurists.' One of those books was *The Aquarian Conspiracy*, authored by Marilyn Ferguson. I was told that it was the 'best reference' to the 'new curriculum' that was coming into our school district. I read the book and decided if the 'future' that Marilyn Ferguson was predicting was in fact going to become a reality, I wanted no part of it. I discovered that this was the 'foundational book' of the 'New Age' movement."

To help the teachers in Littleton become effective change agents, they were required to attend training sessions given by the Strategic Options Initiative. The trainees were requested to read the second, third, and ninth chapters of *The Aquarian Conspiracy*.

Marilyn Ferguson wrote in chapter nine, "You can only have a new society, the visionaries have said, if you change the education of the younger generation. Yet the new society itself is the necessary force for change in education....Of the Aquarian conspirators surveyed, more were involved in education than in any other single category of work.... Tens of thousands of classroom teachers, educational consultants and psychologists, counselors, administrators, researchers, and faculty members engaged in colleges of education have been among the millions engaged in personal transformation."

In other words, American schools like Columbine High have been completely paganized by educators who have adopted the occult philosophy of the Aquarian Conspiracy. It is a philosophy in conflict with Judeo-Christian teachings, and it is a philosophy that opens the door to satanism. It is impossible for a member of the Aquarian

Conspiracy to be indifferent to Christianity. He must oppose it, for Christianity is based on absolute Biblical principles that condemn pagans. That is why the public educrats are so adamantly opposed to any acknowledgment of the Biblical God in the schools.

What happened in Littleton, and what has happened in other schools and will happen in the future, are the results of the rejection of Biblical moral absolutes and the adoption of New Age moral relativism. Paganism is so morally permissive that it could not find a reason to interfere with the two Nazis planning to blow up the school and kill far more students than they actually did in their rampage. The fact that they also killed themselves as part of the process indicates how completely they had given their souls to Satan, the ultimate enemy of the God of the Bible.

It is obvious that no one will blame the schools for anything that happened. The New Age pagan philosophy permeates the public schools, and any child who believes in Biblical religion will be at risk. Yet it was interesting to see how totally bonded the kids at Columbine had become with their school, unable to understand how the school's permissive moral philosophy had made them vulnerable to such murderous attacks.

The two trench coat murderers would have never been able to get away with their behavior in the kind of public schools I attended as a youngster in the 1930s and '40s. In the first place, we had a dress code, which would have made such eccentric dress impossible. We had a principal who read the Twenty-third Psalm from the Bible at assemblies. Student behavior was far more regulated by the rules of discipline. Teachers stuck to their jobs as teachers. They were not interested in our feelings or self-esteem or sexuality. They were not change agents trying to get into our heads with pagan ideas. They respected our religion, our family's values, our individualism. They wanted to improve our lives, not manipulate them. And that's why we loved our teachers and never vandalized our schools. Pity that today's kids can't enjoy the safety and security we had in those days.

CHRISTIAN MARTYRDOM IN COLORADO

One of the most poignant and heartbreaking stories to come out of the Columbine High School massacre is that of seventeen-year-old Cassie Bernall, who had recently pledged to live her life according to Christ's teachings. She wrote, "Now I have given up on everything else — I have found it to be the only way to really know Christ and to experience the mighty power that brought him back to life again, and to find out what it means to suffer and to die with him. So, whatever it takes, I will be one who lives in the fresh newness of life of those who are alive from the dead."

Cassie was one of the students in the school library who faced the killers head-on. She had been reading her Bible when one of the killers confronted her and asked, "Do you believe in God?" She said, "Yes, I believe in God," in a voice strong enough so that her fellow students could hear her. The gunman, in his long black trench coat, laughed. "Why?" he asked mockingly, and then shot her to death.

Cassie had given her life for Christ. It was a terribly tragic end to a young promising life that had just been reborn. And yet, in a way, it sums up the dilemma that many Christians face today in trying to come to terms with our secular culture. As we all know, Biblical religion has been removed from the public schools where Nazi-like, satanic cults can flourish with no opposition from anyone. That is why it has become increasingly dangerous for Christian children to attend public schools. Not only are they subject to anti-Christian secular humanist ideology, which pervades the curriculum, but also to the murderous hatred of young satanists.

Young Christians were also the target of an attack that occurred in December of 1977 at Heath High School in Paducah, Kentucky, where fourteen-year-old Michael Carneal opened fire on a student prayer group that met before classes in the hallway of the school.

Three girls were killed, five wounded, including one girl left para-lyzed. Carneal had a history of heckling the prayer group. He even warned several classmates that "something big is about to happen" and told one student not to go to the prayer group.

Was Michael Carneal a satanist? His hatred of the students in the prayer group indicated a spiritual disturbance so deep that he could not even tolerate the sight of a group of Christian students at prayer. We do not know what kind of a home Carneal came from. But we do know that Biblical religion pervades Kentucky culture. We do not know if Carneal had ever read the Bible or was influenced by satanic teachings. But what is obvious is that he had a murderous hatred of those outwardly Christian students and was motivated to action by that hate.

In October 1997, sixteen-year-old Luke Woodham killed his mother, his ex-girlfriend, and wounded seven others at Pearl High School in Pearl, Mississippi. According to a *Boston Globe* account: "A sobbing Luke Woodham said he remembered getting a butcher knife and seeing his mother's bloody body — all the while, his head ringing with instructions from his satanic mentor, nineteen-year-old Grant Boyette." Apparently, Boyette was the leader of a satanic group plotting to kill students at Pearl High School. "Woodham said he befriended Boyette in January 1997 after Boyette cast a spell from a satanic book. 'We started a satanic group and through the hate in my heart, I used it to try and get vengeance on people and do what he told me to do,' Woodham said."

Meanwhile, teachers, principals, and politicians have reacted to all of this violence in predictable ways. Teachers and counselors offer "conflict resolution" as a means of preventing such killings, as if sa-tanists are interested in resolving their conflicts peacefully. Politicians offer more gun-control legislation, as if the killers hadn't already bro-ken every gun law on the books.

But what are Christian leaders telling their flocks about send-ing Christian children into dangerous public schools? The only well-known Christian leader who has been telling parents for decades to abandon the public schools and put their children in Christian schools or homeschool them is the Rev. R. J. Rushdoony. His book

The Messianic Character of American Education, first published in 1963, revealed the irreconcilable conflict between Christianity and secular humanism that was and still is being waged in the public schools. Rev. Rushdoony predicted that moral chaos in the classroom would in time be the result of that conflict.

There is also the problem with parents. It is hard to believe that the parents of Eric Harris, eighteen, and Dylan Klebold, seventeen, did not know something about what their kids were up to. Last fall the kids had made a sick, hate-filled video with guns. Where were the gun-law fanatics? Klebold's father is known to be a liberal in favor of strong anti-gun laws. It is even probable that the future killers were doing everything in their power to get their parents' attention. For instance, the day before the massacre, a neighbor heard one of the killers smashing glass with a baseball bat in the garage. A neighbor could hear it, but the parents apparently could not. Is it possible that the parents had already given up on their son and wanted nothing to do with him? Or were they simply too busy to notice the strange dress, the Nazi symbols, the guns, the videos?

In any case, it is obvious that all of the remedies being offered by the establishment are not going to solve the spiritual problems that now plague the government schools. The homeschool movement has demonstrated that a growing number of parents have given up on solutions proposed by politicians and educrats and have taken matters into their own hands, protecting their kids and educating them religiously and academically. These kids are safe from murderous satanists, and they are thriving. Why? Because they are getting what children want most: more time with their parents, and in homeschooling they get the maximum.

DEATH EDUCATION
AT COLUMBINE HIGH

On May 22, 1999, the seniors at Columbine High School graduated. They tossed their caps into the air, celebrating their liberation from twelve years of public education where they were indoctrinated in the system's moral and academic chaos and were undoubtedly glad to come out of it alive. Some of their classmates did not. They remembered those who did not, omitting the names of the two perpetrators of the massacre who were also supposed to graduate that weekend. Instead, those two chose death.

Which brings us to the subject of death education. Death education has been a part of the progressive curriculum in virtually every public school in America for at least the last fifteen years. Yet no one in the establishment, let alone the U.S. Department of Education, has sought to find out what death education is doing to the minds and souls of the millions of children who are subjected to it. But we do have plenty of anecdotal information on hand.

For example, back in 1985, Tara Becker, a student from Columbine High, went to a pro-family conference in Colorado to tell the attendees about death education at the school and the effect it had on her. Jayne Schindler, who heard Tara's testimony, reported:

> Tara brought with her a booklet she had helped to compile
> for one of her school classes. This booklet was called "Mas-
> querade" and was full of subliminal pictures and prose. Tara
> explained how she had been taught to use the hidden, double
> meaning, subliminals and how she had focused so much of
> her time and attention on death that she, herself, had tried to
> commit suicide.

A video was made of Tara's testimony and distributed nationwide by Eagle Forum. The tape was aired on British television, and the

The Atlantic Monthly did a feature story based on it. The producers at *20/20* saw the video and decided to do a segment on death education, which was aired in 1990. I remember that video very well because I was called by the freelance writer who was working on the story and sent her some of the newsletters I had written on the subject.

Schindler wrote, "Tara explained that the subject of death was integrated into many of the courses at her high school. She said that death was made to look glamorous, that living was hard, and that re-incarnation would solve their problems. Students were told that they would always return to a much better life form. They would return to the 'Oversoul' and become like God.

"After one of the students at her school committed suicide, a 'suicide talking day' was held and every class was to talk about death. Class assignments were for students to write their own obituaries and suicide notes. They were told to trust their own judgment in choos-ing whether to live or die."

So Tara began to think of suicide as a means of solving some of her problems. She thought of liberating her spirit from enslavement to her body. She says she also wanted to die to help relieve the planet of overpopulation. These were a few of the crazy thoughts put into her head by her "educators." God knows what kind of equally crazy thoughts were put into the heads of the two killers at Columbine.

Fortunately, Tara survived death education at Columbine High and lived to talk about it. But thousands of students have committed suicide all across America, and no one in Washington has even both-ered to hold a hearing on the subject. It is now assumed that teenage suicide is as natural as burgers and fries. It's just one of those things that teenagers now do in America.

But what seems to be happening as death education becomes more and more sophisticated is that many of these teenagers with the suicidal urge now want to take some of their teachers and classmates with them. After all, reincarnation is an equal opportunity concept. It's for everybody.

How long has this been going on? Here are some excerpts from an article entitled "Development Opportunities for Teachers of Death Education" published in *The Clearing House* in May 1989.

This article reaffirms the need for death education and offers some methods for improving pedagogical skills of teachers.

A task force appointed by the president of the Association for Death Education and Counseling ... is charged to (1) carry out a study of the current state of death education in U.S. schools, (2) make recommendations for the ideal K–12 curriculum in death education, and (3) make recommendations for minimal knowledge, skills, and attitudes that teachers should possess before attempting to teach death education to children....

Although we can assume that most pedagogical efforts are sound, recent examples have surfaced, depicting miseducation and ill handling of attempts to address dimensions of dying and death. Consider the following items from the *Dallas Morning Press*:

"Some have blamed death education classes for the suicides of two students who attended courses in Illinois and Missouri. Other students have suffered traumatic reactions. Minimally trained or untrained teachers have asked first graders to make model coffins out of shoe boxes; other students have been instructed to sit in coffins, measure themselves for caskets, list ten ways of dying (including violent death), attend an embalming and touch an undraped corpse."

Certainly mistakes do occur in many instructional settings and some minimally trained teachers may, on occasion, handle situations inappropriately. But let us hope that the above examples are rare and that effective death education is the norm in our schools throughout America.

There you have it. A plea made more than ten years ago for "effective death education," whatever that is. What is "effective" death education? Can the educators tell us? What about simply eliminating death education? But that won't happen, because if we did, we'd have to get rid of values clarification, sensitivity training, transcendental meditation, out-of-body experience, magic circles, Outcome Based Education, drug ed, sex ed, suicide ed, and now massacre ed.

Incidentally, the National Education Association has played an active role in promoting death education. It sponsored the writing and publication of *Death and Dying Education* by Professor Richard O. Ulin of the University of Massachusetts. The book, written in 1978, includes an eighteen-week syllabus for the death educator.

Rev. R. J. Rushdoony has written, "Humanistic education is the institutionalized love of death." Meanwhile, the best the schools and President Clinton can offer the kids is grief counseling and conflict resolution by trained counselors who will have a lot more work to do in the future.

BACK TO SCHOOL AT COLUMBINE

On Monday, August 16, students returned to Columbine High for their fall 1999 semester. During the summer, workers patched the bullet holes, remodeled the cafeteria, repainted it blue and green, and added new furnishings and tile. As yet, officials have not decided what they want to do about the library, where most of the carnage took place. They've gotten rid of the bloody carpet and sealed off the room where most of the students were murdered and where the two killers killed themselves. A temporary library will be housed in modular classrooms.

In many respects, that sealed-off library can be viewed as a reminder of the nihilist philosophy that pervades the curriculum at Columbine. Should that room ever be reopened, we can expect that the spirits of the dead students and their murderers will haunt its atmosphere. School officials may remodel it, repaint it, replace the furniture, remove the books that silently witnessed the satanic orgy of murder, but school officials will never be able to get rid of the haunting spirits.

If the school authorities had any sense, they'd turn that room into a shrine to the dead, with pictures of the students and their killers, newspaper and magazine clippings, videos, and poems by students. They should turn it into a miniature holocaust museum so that no one forgets what happened at Columbine High on April 20, 1999.

Having studied and written about American education for the last thirty years, I'm afraid that I see in Columbine High a microcosm of everything that is wrong in American education and culture today. It represents the full flower of satanic humanism with death education permeating the entire curriculum and infecting every child with its deadly virus of gloom, depression, and suicide. It easily leads many impressionable youngsters into the Goth subculture with its obsession with death.

If you want to know what Goth is all about, just look it up on the Internet and you'll be amazed at what you'll find. For example, there is an International Goth Club Listing with over 260 clubs worldwide. They have such names as Death Guild, Necropolis, Perversion, Bar Sinister, Coven 13, Sin Klub, Delerium, Dark Carnival, Dementia, The Morgue, The Mausoleum, Death Rattle, Murder, The Dark Side, The Inferno, just to mention a few.

Their music is provided by such bands as Switchblade Symphony, Covenant, Bauhaus, UK Decay, Southern Death Cult, Alien Sex Fiend, Christian Death, Cradle of Filth, Morbid Angel, Fear Factory, etc. There is a fascination with vampires, witchcraft, and the occult. At a website entitled "Suburban Goths" we are told:

> Goth is a state of mind. In fact it is quite individualistic. If you ask a number of Goths for their definition of Gothic each will be different yet similar in theme. Some will tell you Gothic is a way of life embracing death and darkness — to accept death as a part of life and bring themselves not to fear it. Some will say it is a style characterized by the use of desolate or remote settings and macabre, mysterious and violent incidents.

Satanism gained its entry into the public school through death education. It has led many students to embrace death and darkness as a way of life. And the obsession can become so strong that even an orgy of murder can't fully satisfy the satanic lust for destruction. That is why on the first day back at Columbine High two one-inch swastikas were found scratched into a freshly painted stall in a girl's restroom, another was found in a boy's restroom, and a fourth was scratched into a brick wall outside the school.

Yet Christian parents will continue to send their sons and daughters into Satan's territory because they are so totally confused by what is going on that they refuse to believe that their lives are being lived on the edge of disaster. Their own Christian faith is so weak and riddled with doubt that they cannot see evil at work even when it hits them in the face. They blame the murders not on satanic forces, but on guns, which the vast majority of gun-owners use for sport or self-protection.

Meanwhile, members of the Trench Coat Mafia, the student group that Eric Harris and Dylan Klebold hung out with, have returned to Columbine along with their classmates. A photo and message from the Trench Coat Mafia appeared in the 1998 Columbine High School yearbook. The message read:

> We are Josh, Joe, Chris, Horst, Chuck, Brian, Pauline, Nicole, Kristen, Krista, plus Tad, Alex, Cory. Who says we're different. Insanity's healthy! Remember rocking parties at Kristen's, foos-ball at Joe's, and fencing at Christopher's! Stay alive, stay different, stay crazy! Oh, and stay away from Cream Soda!!
>
> Love Always, The Chicks.

Nicole, a senior, told a reporter, "I know, and all my friends know, I had nothing to do with it [the shooting]. If they want to tease me for having a good time with Harris and Klebold, fine.... I consider them my friends."

The mother of a former Trench Coat Mafia member told a reporter that she encouraged her son, eighteen, to return to Columbine. He had dropped out before Christmas because he said the schoolwork was not challenging. "Sometimes, what you imagine is going to happen is just a whole lot worse," she said. "I'm just tickled to pieces he wants to go back. He's at home at Columbine."

Even when kids want to get away from the Columbines of America, their parents will insist that they stay. Why would a parent be "tickled to pieces" to see her son go back into the scene of a massacre and claim that he's "at home" there?

Meanwhile, as liberals, led by President Clinton, carry on their hysterical crusade against guns, the authorities at Columbine have beefed up security with more armed guards, sixteen extra surveillance cameras, and a requirement that students wear ID badges. Satan is laughing all the way to the (blood) bank.

MULTICULTURALISM

I f it weren't for our government school system, multiculturalism would hardly be an issue in American education today. But because a government school system suggests uniformity of curriculum and standards, the issue has always been whose standards, whose curriculum, whose values are to be advanced by the education system?

Back in the 1840s and 50s, in the early days of government education, there was already an intense dispute between Protestants and Catholics over which religious doctrine would be promulgated in the schools. The Protestants wanted a nonsectarian Christianity that virtually every Protestant sect could agree upon.

But the Catholics were afraid that their children would be lost to a nonsectarian Protestantism. They tried to get the legislatures to vote for Catholic public schools, but that idea was rejected by the Protestant majority because they feared that permitting Catholics to have their own state-funded public schools would encourage Methodists, Baptists, Presbyterians, and other Protestant sects to demand publicly funded schools for their own sects. It was this dispute, incidentally, which set the stage for the gradual removal of Biblical religion from the public schools entirely.

And so the only alternative left to the Catholics was to create their own private parochial system for their own children financed out of their own resources. Over the years the Catholic parochial schools gained a reputation for high academic standards and strong religious instruction. And the children who emerged from these schools were no less patriotic, no less American than the children from the public schools. That's how multiculturalism was handled in those days. It wasn't labeled multiculturalism. It was a matter of religious freedom, educational freedom, and parental rights.

In the decades following the Civil War, the Southern states practiced their own kind of social and educational multiculturalism. Blacks attended all-black schools administered by black principals. They were taught by black teachers who belonged to an all-black professional teachers' association. The teams were black, the glee clubs were black, and the bands were black. All of that ended with the U.S. Supreme Court's ruling mandating forced integration in 1971 to achieve the theoretically beneficial goal of racial balance.

Was education for blacks in the South improved by forced integration? Unfortunately not. And it had nothing to do with race. When reading instruction methods were changed in the early 1930s from alphabetic phonics to look-say, all children, regardless of race, began to experience reading difficulties. That was the beginning of the general dumbing down of the American people in the interests of progressive socialist goals. The result over the years has been a serious decline in academic performance and literacy throughout the American government school system.

This is tragic, for the literacy statistics from 1890 to 1930 showed a steady improvement in literacy among blacks. For example, in 1890, the illiteracy rate among blacks was 57.1 percent; in 1900 it was 44.5 percent; in 1910 it was 30.4 percent; in 1920 it was 22.9 percent; in 1930 it was 16.3 percent. Had children continued to be taught to read by intensive, systematic phonics, the illiteracy rate among blacks today would surely be close to zero. But with look-say, the statistics began to go in the other direction. Today, black functional illiteracy now stands at close to 50 percent. (*School and Society*, 11/19/21 p. 466; 4/9/32, p. 489.)

The dumbing down of America has affected all races and social groups in our population. In the black and Hispanic communities, however, the rate of functional illiteracy is now so high that thousands of these young adults have no employable skills and are ripe for recruitment in the illicit drug trade, in petty crime, in gangs addicted to violence. These young adults make up the hard core of our economic underclass that plagues America's inner cities. Mind you, all of them attended public schools, and all of them emerged knowing virtually nothing: they can't read, they can't write, they can't spell, and they can barely speak standard English. As for arithmetic, they learn that on the streets dealing drugs.

But what most Americans do not realize is that there is probably just as much functional illiteracy among the white middle class.

Among whites, that condition is known as dyslexia requiring expensive tutoring and remediation. But there are hundreds of thousands of white Americans who do not read for pleasure because it is too difficult for them. That's the legacy of look-say. And the market has accommodated itself to this situation. If you look at the novels that sell millions of copies, particularly the very popular romance novels, you will notice that they do not tax the reader very heavily. The sentences are short, there are not too many multisyllabic words. In fact, they are generally written at a fourth through sixth grade level.

Multiculturalism has nothing to do with the improvement of academic performance. It is simply part of the plan to use the public schools for political and psychological purposes rather than for academic ones. While multiculturalism doesn't necessarily make anyone dumber, it creates tension, confusion, and conflict within the education system. And that is why it is there: to create the tension and conflict change agents need to create a fertile ground for further revolutionary change.

Our humanist educators now consider multiculturalism to be so important that the National Council for Accreditation of Teacher Education (NCATE) has given it a very prominent place in teacher education programs. The NCATE's publication, *Standards for the Accreditation of Teacher Education* (July 1982) stated:

> Multicultural education is preparation for the social, political, and economic realities that individuals experience in culturally diverse and complex human encounters.... This preparation provides a process by which an individual develops competencies for perceiving, believing, evaluating, and behaving in differential cultural settings.

> Provision should be made for instruction in multicultural education in teacher education programs. Multicultural education should receive attention in courses, seminars, directed readings, laboratory and clinical experiences, practicum, and other types of field exercises.

> Multicultural education should include, but would not be limited to experiences which: (1) promote analytical and

evaluative abilities to confront issues such as participatory democracy, racism and sexism, and the parity of power; (2) develop skills for values clarification including the study of the manifest and latent transmission of values; (3) examine the dynamics of diverse cultures and the implications for developing teaching strategies; and (4) examine linguistic variations and diverse learning styles as a basis for the development of appropriate teaching strategies.

In other words, there is quite a socio-political agenda behind multiculturalism. Notice that teachers should be able to confront such issues as "participatory democracy" and "the parity of power." Both phrases are code words for socialism. The educators know they cannot use the word "socialism" anymore, because socialism, wherever tried, has proved to be a total failure, leading to totalitarianism, despotism, slavery, and national impoverishment. They have invented other ways to convey to their brethren what they mean.

Indeed, it may seem irrational for anyone to want a socialist society with the evidence we now have that it doesn't work. So why do the educators want it? I think that what they want is control over society. What they want is power to control people, power to force people to do what they, the elite, want. The environmental movement best represents their goal: an economy controlled by the environmentalists. I don't think they care whether or not it is called socialism. That's why phrases like participatory democracy, or industrial democracy, or economic justice are readily acceptable and understood by socialists because they convey the same philosophy of government control of the economy by a university-trained, politically correct elite.

Also notice that multiculturalism has something to do with "values clarification" and "the study of the manifest and latent transmission of values." Teachers must know how to transmit values, overtly and covertly, directly and indirectly. But whose values are they talking about? The word "latent" is interesting. The dictionary defines latent as "present but invisible or inactive; lying hidden and undeveloped within a person or things, as a quality or power. ...latent applies to that which exists but is as yet concealed or unrevealed." In other words, the concealed or hidden transmission of values.

As for "linguistic variations," that no doubt refers to black English, which is supposed to represent a cultural value. Actually, the decline in speech among young blacks is not the result of a positive cultural development or an attempt to return to the language of their African ancestors. It is the result of several generations of miseducation in which the teaching of reading by the sight method instead of the phonetic method has led to a degeneration of speech not only among blacks but among whites also. Young Americans today use a shrunken vocabulary based on an inability to read or understand many multisyllabic words. However, among blacks the degeneration of speech has led to the development of a new inner-city dialect that lends itself to rap speech, which has been transformed into a very popular genre of musical entertainment. When multiculturalists speak of linguistic variations, they are trying to lend cultural legitimacy to the new black dialect.

It is interesting to note that Africans in Africa speak English far better and more correctly than many American blacks. You notice this whenever Africans are interviewed on television. They speak standard English, sometimes with a slight accent, but they do not speak what we call black English. Yet these Africans are much closer to their tribal roots and languages than American blacks whose ancestors were brought to this country more than 150 years ago.

But there is much more to multiculturalism than the simple acknowledgment of cultural or ethnic diversity. A rather comprehensive review of multiculturalism was given in the Spring 1984 issue of *Theory Into Practice*, the journal of the College of Education at Ohio State University. That issue contains thirteen articles on multicultural education covering many aspects of the subject.

Multiculturalism is based on the notion that the traditional Christian model of American values based on Biblical teachings is no longer valid as the model to be held up to children in the public schools. These values are generally associated with white, Anglo-Saxon Protestant culture, usually referred to as WASP culture by its critics. The Founding Fathers represented the finest expression of this model; and, for most of our national existence, this model taught generations of young Americans, including the children of immigrants, what an American was.

As a child of immigrant parents I was more than happy to emulate that American model. I had no interest in the country my parents came from. In the public school I attended in New York City in the early 1930s, a picture of George Washington hung in virtually every classroom. My parents wanted me to become an American, and I had no desire to become anything else. Even though I was brought up in the Jewish religion, it created no obstacle to being a full-fledged American. And even though my parents spoke English with a foreign accent, they loved America very deeply. I never heard my parents utter a single word of complaint about this country. They thanked God that America existed and took great pride in their citizenship. In those days, the public schools made no bones about their mission to make Americans out of the children of immigrants.

Sad to say, this is no longer true. And it isn't only the children of immigrants who are suffering as a result. Our humanist educators believe that our Bible-based culture is in decline and is not being replaced by another dominant model. In fact, the American Association of Colleges for Teacher Education (AACTE) statement on multicultural education is entitled "No One Model American." *Ergo*, many models will take its place.

A multicultural society, they say, is one made up of many equally valid ideals that can serve as equally valid models for young Americans. If this is the case, then who is the model that black American youths are to emulate? Martin Luther King, Jr.? Jesse Jackson? Malcolm X? Bill Cosby? Michael Jackson? And who are white American youths to emulate? President Clinton, Hillary Clinton, Ronald Reagan, or some rock star? No one is required any longer to conform to the once dominant Christian ideal, and the public schools are now *required* to convey this message to their students.

The public school as an Americanizing institution, providing a common body of values for all American children, no longer exists. According to Charles A. Tesconi, dean of the College of Education at the University of Vermont:

> We all know by now that homogeneity has not and does not characterize American society. We know how great a myth the

"melting pot" turned out to be.... American society, then, is best characterized as a mosaic of an extensive, highly diverse array of cultural elements.

As a descriptor, multiculturalism points to a condition of numerous life-styles, values, and belief systems.

Ah, so here is a new component in multiculturalism: we are not only dealing with ethnic and racial diversity but with alternative lifestyles, values, and belief systems. How is multiculturalism, therefore, to be taught, and what will be its desired results? Professor Tesconi wrote:

> By treating diverse cultural groups and ways of life as equally legitimate, and by teaching about them in positive ways, legitimizing differences through various education policies and practices, self-understanding and harmony, and equal opportunity are promoted.

Thus multicultural education teaches the tolerant acceptance of different lifestyles, values and belief systems, thereby legitimizing moral diversity. The concept of moral diversity directly contradicts the Biblical concept of moral absolutes on which this nation was founded. It also leads to judicial chaos. A nation's courts cannot be run by two mutually exclusive moral codes.

The current battle over abortion is a direct result of this judicial confusion. The U.S. Supreme Court adopted a humanist moral code in the 1970s, thereby negating our Bible-based moral code, which has been the foundation of this nation's legal system from the very beginning. The result is the making of a cultural civil war. Pro-lifers want to restore the Bible-based moral code; the abortionists want the humanist moral revolution to continue going forward. President Clinton has vowed to choose a Supreme Court nominee who will consolidate the humanist moral revolution.

Our public schools, in order to be accredited, are now required to teach that there are no *moral* absolutes, that every individual through a process of values clarification has the right to *freely* choose his morals, and that *ethics* are situational. The result has been moral anarchy, moral confusion, moral decline, moral disintegration, and moral civil war. No nation can tolerate the confusion of two conflict-ing moral codes in its courts. Multiculturalism is a recipe for civil strife, for it requires the people to accept the impossible.

What all of this means in practical terms is that American pub-lic schools are no longer to be used to inculcate a common set of moral and spiritual values based on our Biblical heritage, but are to be used to promote a plethora of competing values systems, with Biblical Christian values cleverly excluded from competition because they violate the sacred separation of church and state. In other words, the public school is now a marketplace of competing pagan and anti-Christian belief systems. The students have a *choice*, but the market is rigged. That, in a nutshell, is how multiculturalism works to un-dermine our Judeo-Christian heritage.

How *is* multicultural education taught? It is not a course that is taught separately from the rest of the subject matter. It is, in reality, a worldview which, in the words of Theresa E. McCormick, specialist in multicultural education at Emporia State University, "must per-meate the total educational environment."

That means that multicultural education, in the words of Sandra B. DeCosta, associate professor at West Virginia University, "must be carefully planned, organized, and integrated into all the subject areas. But most emphatically it must begin when children first enter school."

Thus it is now official policy in the government schools to in-culcate moral anarchy in American children beginning with grade one. Is it therefore any wonder that we read of more and more atro-cious crimes being committed by teenagers and even pre-teenagers? It is now official policy of the government schools to deny that there exists a common value system known as Americanism — unless by Americanism you mean the freedom to do your own thing regardless of the consequences.

For example, most Americans have been willing to leave homo-sexuals alone to pursue their own life-styles, as long as their behavior didn't interfere with the lives of non-homosexuals. But homosexual promiscuity has produced the AIDS plague that, through contami-nated blood transfusions, has jeopardized the health of thousands of non-gay Americans. And what about the innocent children born with AIDS? Who takes responsibility for their suffering and truncated lives?

In other words, there is a price to be paid for toleration of perversion, for legitimizing a lifestyle that threatens the health of an entire nation. A society cannot permit the free exercise of promiscuous perversion without being affected by it in unexpected, costly, and deadly ways. There is a reason why homosexuality is forbidden in the Bible. And we are just now finding out why.

But the multicultural juggernaut goes on, and there are now children's books to help children understand and tolerate homosexuality. In fact, the full effects of multiculturalism can be found in today's primary grade textbooks, where you have racial and ethnic diversity portrayed in reading primers, with women construction workers and male kindergarten teachers, stories about witchcraft, the occult, pagan ceremonies, Eastern religion and whatever else is necessary to convey the idea of moral diversity.

Despite the efforts of the schools to de-emphasize Americanism, we know that Americanism exists and does constitute the basis of American consciousness: the conviction that this nation was created with God's help and God's blessings to demonstrate to the world that with the true God all good things are possible, and that without Him we will be consigned to the same tyranny and misery that now afflicts the millions who live under paganism or atheistic communism.

During the celebration of the 100th anniversary of the Statue of Liberty, that concept of Americanism was expressed over and over again in song and speech in three simple words: God Bless America. Those three words acknowledge the existence, efficacy, and sovereignty of the God of the Bible. They express the essence of Americanism, the peculiar consciousness that makes us different from other peoples.

Even President Clinton says "God Bless You" or "God Bless America" at the ends of his speeches. As much as the humanists would like to get rid of every public acknowledgment of the existence of God, they cannot succeed as long as that acknowledgment rises spontaneously from the hearts of the American people.

While that consciousness of God's blessings was given to us by our Founding Fathers who, for the most part, were indeed white, Anglo-Saxon Protestants, one does not have to be white, Anglo-Saxon, or even Protestant to accept it. There are many blacks, Hispanics, Latins, Slavs, Catholics, Jews, etc., who gladly accept it.

Becoming an American does not mean aping WASPs. It never did, and it never will. It means accepting the essence of what the Founding Fathers stood for and died for. That essence is founded on Biblical principles that include the concept of moral absolutes. The public schools now presume that blacks, Hispanics, native Americans, Asians, and other immigrant children are incapable of understanding or unwilling to accept the philosophy of the Founding Fathers. Therefore they won't even teach it to them. It is a crime to deprive young Americans and immigrant children of the great Biblical heritage that has made this nation the envy of the world. And yet the Bible, the very book on which the President places his hand when he takes his oath of office, is kept out of our public schools.

The Bible is the foundation of that way of life we call Americanism. In fact, one can hardly be considered educated unless one knows the Bible. Multiculturalism is really nothing more than a new form of anti-Americanism.

What kind of Americans will the public schools turn out? Americans ignorant of their nation's founding principles, incapable of defending their country against foreign ideologies, adrift in a sea of moral and cultural anarchy, at the mercy of fears, slogans, and terrorist blackmail. The simple truth is that the ultimate purpose of multiculturalism is to wean the American people away from patriotism.

In fact, multiculturalism is an all-important steppingstone to globalism, that concept of a future world government, which the public schools are now promoting more aggressively than ever. In an article entitled "Multicultural Education and Global Education: A Possible Merger," Donna J. Cole of Wittenberg University wrote:

> A multiculturalized global education would address the basic concern of where the individual fits into the mosaic of humanity and where others fit in the same mosaic.... It would

aid students in understanding that our membership in groups affects our values and attitudes....It would assist students in recognizing the need to be flexible and adjustable citizens in a rapidly changing world.

The National Education Association (NEA) of course endorses multicultural-global education. Its resolution on the subject states:

> The National Education Association believes that multicultural-global education is a way of helping every student perceive the cultural diversity of the U.S. citizenry so that children of many races may develop pride in their own cultural legacy, awaken to the ideals embodied in the cultures of their neighbors, and develop an appreciation of the common humanity shared by all peoples of the earth.

Notice that the NEA recognizes no American culture that the student may take pride in. He is to take pride in his own racial "cultural legacy" and learn to appreciate the cultures of others, but nowhere in sight is there an indigenous culture based on peculiarly American values to appreciate, take pride in, or identify with.

The purpose of globalism is to prepare young Americans to accept as inevitable and desirable a world socialist government in which American national sovereignty will be voluntarily surrendered for the greater good of "world peace and brotherhood." Social studies textbooks have been written to deliberately play down American patriotism and national pride known as "ethnocentrism" in order to prepare young Americans for world citizenship.

The current strong movement to replace the traditional public school curriculum with a radical new plan known as Outcome Based Education is a further attempt to move the American public school in the direction of multicultural world government. It calls for a curriculum that emphasizes world citizenship through multicultural awareness.

Much of the current pressure for multiculturalism is coming from black educators who deplore the education system's lingering Eurocentric perspective and feel that the self-esteem of young blacks needs bolstering by an emphasis on black achievement. Apparently, according to these educators, blacks cannot identify with American achievement in general. Thus we read in the February 1993 issue of the *Phi Delta Kappan* magazine:

> The Fourth of July is a holiday that commemorates America's freedom from British domination. When America's first Independence Day was celebrated in 1776, African-Americans were not independent; they were not even citizens; they were slaves.

> These issues clearly illustrate the need for an Afrocentric, multicultural curriculum. Whether the subject is history, science, or literature, the experiences of all cultures involved must be equally recognized and legitimized. Such a curriculum would embrace the perspectives of many cultures....

> Everyone is now taught about the great civilizations of Rome and Greece, but how many people learn about the empires of Ethiopia and Ghana?... A strictly Eurocentric perspective will not properly prepare students for a successful future in a multicultural world....

> All students would benefit from an Afrocentric, multicultural curriculum.... African-American students would finally inherit a legacy of excellence and develop confidence, knowing that they too are capable of achieving greatness. Our society today is multicultural. We must, therefore, foster a greater awareness, appreciation, and acknowledgment of the achievements of the many instead of the few.

That's the kind of thinking that is readily accepted in educational journals as legitimate opinion. I have yet to read in any professional educational journal the opinions of a Christian on these matters. Although Christians make up about 85 percent of the population in America, their views are relegated to the educational incinerator.

I wonder if that writer in the *Phi Delta Kappan* would be willing for a course to be taught about the Ethiopian and Ghanaian empires that told the whole truth about those civilizations, that they practiced slavery, female subjugation, cannibalism, genocide, human sacrifice, and despotic rule. In fact, the idea of the noble savage, which the writer seems to espouse, is a product of white idealism and white guilt. It was Jean-Jacques Rousseau, the French apostle of the Enlightenment, who promulgated that false idea that persists unfortunately in the minds of some black writers despite overwhelming evidence to the contrary.

Man's sinful nature extends throughout the whole of the human race. No one is exempt, neither white, nor black, nor Asian. That is why multiculturalism as an educational doctrine will produce nothing but confusion and demoralization. It is based on the fantasy that American culture is basically evil and everybody else's culture is basically good.

Multiculturalism is really nothing more than a transition stage in the changeover from one dominant culture to another. America is moving from a dominant Christian culture to a dominant humanist-pagan culture. The transition is usually marked by increasing conflict between the advocates of the two opposing worldviews. We see these conflicts being waged in many countries on a far bloodier scale: in Lebanon between Christians and Moslems, in Bosnia between Moslems and Christians, in Israel between Jews and Arabs, in India between Hindus and Moslems, in Armenia between Christians and Moslems, in South Africa between blacks and whites and between Christian blacks and Marxist blacks.

American Christians, for the most part, have lost control over American cultural institutions. All of our public schools, all of our state universities and colleges, and most of our private universities and colleges are now totally and irrevocably in the hands of anti-Christian humanists. Their control of our educational institutions virtually guarantees their dominance over the culture, unless Christians can develop a strategy to regain control over the education of Christian children. It is the Christian patronage of the public school that is permitting the humanists to win the cultural war. The tide of that war could be turned tomorrow if Christians would remove their children from the public schools and put them in private Christian schools or homeschools where they could be taught Biblical principles.

It is the duty and responsibility of Christian leaders to stop the wholesale paganization of Christian youth. We should take our lesson from the Catholics of the 1850s who realized that they had no choice but to abandon the public schools for educational institutions of their own if they were to preserve Catholic culture for the next hundred years.

Their success indicates that it can be done if a resolute community is mobilized by a resolute leadership. The fact that thousands of Christian parents are already involved in homeschooling indicates that they are not waiting for this resolute leadership to arise. But one of these days Christians will have to decide whether or not to maintain the Christian character of American civilization or give it up. Only a well-informed community, aware of the dire consequences of surrender, will be able to make the right decision.

THE AMERICAN REVOLUTION GOES ON

There is much disappointment these days among conservatives who have or haven't expected the new Bush administration and conservatives in Congress to reverse the liberal drive toward socialism and global government. The Jeffords defection, which turned the Senate over to the Democrats, was like a punch to the stomach.

This reliance on politicians to bring about a conservative millennium is not only misplaced, but delusional. You have to go outside Congress and the political arena to find where the real freedom revolution is taking place: in the homeschool movement. There is no other movement in America that has done more to recapture the spirit of American freedom than homeschooling.

Homeschoolers are, without question, revolutionary. They are making a clean break with the statist institution of government education. It is government-owned and controlled education that is the very foundation of the secular state, which exerts its power by molding the minds of its youngest citizens to serve the mythical state.

The Founding Fathers never created a "state" that had certain mystical powers over its citizens. That kind of state was an idea conceived by the German philosopher Georg Wilhelm Friedrich Hegel (1770–1831), a pantheist, who saw the state as God on earth. The Germans have long had a rather mystical view of the state and its power over the lives of its people.

In America the Hegelian state idea, introduced in this country by Harvard intellectuals and educators, has evolved into something that simply cannot be made compatible with the American idea of government, which is well stated in our Declaration of Independence. That document tells us that the purpose of government is to secure the unalienable rights of the people, rights to life, liberty and the pursuit of happiness. This is a philosophy of government more

165

compatible with the Bible than with Hegel. When American courts speak of a compelling state interest in education without defining the state, or what is meant by compelling, or education, the assumption is that Americans now regard the state as some sort of higher godlike power that must be served. The state they are talking about is the mystical Hegelian state.

What we have in America is a government, not a "state" in the Hegelian sense. We have a government run by men who must conform to a Constitution, which places limits on what the government can do. There are no limits on what the Hegelian state can do, a fact tragically demonstrated during the Nazi era, when the state became a persecutor and mass murderer of its own citizens.

In addition, we have a constitutional republic, not a democracy. A democracy is simply majority rule. A republic, through its written constitution, limits what the majority can do to the minority. Representatives, elected by the citizenry, are obliged to adhere to the limits placed on them by the Constitution.

Most Americans speak of our government as a democracy. They have virtually no understanding of the profound difference between a democracy and a constitutional republic. This gross lack of understanding is the work of our statist education system, which has a vested interest in keeping Americans ignorant of the true role of limited government. The mystical "will of the people" is now what is considered to be the essence of American democracy. The "will of the people," often invoked by liberal politicians, has become the sacred mantra of the liberal secular state, as long as the "will of the people" can be manipulated by the liberal-dominated media.

The homeschool revolution was started by Christians who recognized the implicit conflict between Biblical religion and secular humanism. When it became obvious to them that the government schools had been thoroughly captured by the humanists, these parents had no choice but to remove their children from them. And inasmuch as many private schools have been greatly influenced by humanist philosophy, these Christian parents found it necessary to do the educating themselves. Also, many of them were strongly motivated to follow God's commandments concerning the education of children as given in Deuteronomy 6.

While religion was the primary moving force behind the early homeschoolers, they were also well aware of the academic decline within the public schools, which no longer knew how to teach such basic subjects as reading or arithmetic. After all, it was in April 1983 that the National Commission on Excellence in Education issued its now historic report, stating: "If an unfriendly foreign power had attempted to impose on America the mediocre education performance that exists today, we might well have viewed it as an act of war. As it stands, we have allowed this to happen to ourselves." Eighteen years later, the schools are probably worse than they were in 1983.

These early homeschoolers were the pioneers in the movement. They were generally well-educated orthodox Christians who understood the political and cultural forces at work and were willing to take the necessary steps to guard their children against the growing moral and academic chaos in the public schools. In those days they were a tiny minority, and they tended to keep low profiles. However, whenever they were dragged into court by local superintendents, who asserted implicitly that the children were owned by the state, Christian leaders like the late Rev. Rousas J. Rushdoony were called by the parents to defend their God-given right and their God-commanded duty to educate their children at home. It was Rev. Rushdoony's staunch Biblical defense of Christian parental responsibilities that provided a moral and spiritual backbone to the Christian homeschool movement.

Those were the days before the creation of the Home School Legal Defense Association. The pioneers, like the Founding Fathers, tended to be strong people, willing to accept the consequences of their actions, willing to fight for their right to control and minister their own children's education. The law and tradition were basically on their side. There were no federal laws forbidding homeschooling. In fact, education was not even mentioned in the U.S. Constitution. Also, most state compulsory school attendance laws provided room for exemptions.

Nevertheless, here and there, local judges, ignoring the Constitution, but backed by the district's education establishment, ordered local police to drag children away from their parents in conformity with the state's supposed compelling interest in education. That's what happened in Payette County, Idaho, in 1985. In such cases, the public and even the liberal media tended to sympathize with the homeschoolers. News pictures of perfectly decent children being dragged away from their parents were not good public relations for the school authorities.

Some parents actually went to jail. That was the case with Sharon and Ed Pangelinan, who spent 132 days in jail in Morgan County, Alabama, in 1985, because they had decided to homeschool their children without the school district's approval and refused to turn their children over to the state authorities when ordered. Again, jailing Christian parents for homeschooling did not make good PR for state officials.

Two years later, after the ordeal was over, Sharon Pangelinan was asked why she and her husband didn't take the children and leave Alabama. She wrote:

> That question was asked of us over and over before the trial. (And would continue to be asked during our time in jail, and even after we were released.) We answered the question the same way, over and over again. We don't want to be separated from our children at all. But if we run away, we teach them that courage has no part in liberty. If what you're doing is right, according to Scripture, then you don't run away. Fighting against oppression is indeed Scriptural, especially when it concerns the family.

That is the kind of courage and spiritual strength that undergirded the pioneers of the homeschool movement.

In 1983, three homeschooling lawyers formed the Home School Legal Defense Association, "born out of the need to defend the growing number of home school families in each of our respective communities," wrote Michael Farris, former president of HSLDA, who is also an ordained Baptist minister. Today, thousands of homeschoolers from all fifty states are members of HSLDA, which offers legal services to homeschooling families who experience legal difficulties in their communities. The HSLDA has also become a viable lobby in Congress, bringing the homeschool revolution into the offices of our lawmakers.

In 1999, Michael Farris and his colleagues founded Patrick Henry College, dedicated to educating young Americans in the principles of constitutional government so that the graduates can pursue careers that honor the ideals of our Founding Fathers. And that is what is needed in government, men and women who understand the limits the Constitution places on lawmakers.

Today, the homeschool movement is thriving in a manner that would have been inconceivable twenty years ago. State homeschool organizations now have to rent large convention centers in which to hold their annual conventions, which draw thousands of parents. What we've learned is that there is more to homeschooling than merely removing one's children from the morally corrupt public schools. There is now the sense that the new family lifestyle, which is centered around home education, is highly desirable because of the positive bonding it fosters between parents and children. This is a particular blessing for the Christian family that seeks to live in conformity with Biblical values, which are readily imparted to their children.

While the early homeschoolers were the pioneers, the families that followed were the settlers. They created the state organizations, support groups, magazines, books, and curricula that have evolved into what one can call the homeschool academic and political establishment. While they have a long way to go before they can equal the National Education Association in political clout, the exponential growth of the homeschool movement assures that its influence will be increasingly felt in the state legislatures and congresses of tomorrow.

Today's newcomers to homeschooling are more like refugees, fleeing the failed government schools with their Columbines, academic confusion, moral corruption, and anti-Christian bias. The refugees eagerly seek help from the settlers, who are more than happy to provide it. But we should not assume that the struggle for educational freedom is anywhere near completion. The vast majority of Christians still put their children in public schools, thus justifying their continued existence and involuntary support by the taxpayer. Also, many parents are seeking salvation in other statist programs, such as charter schools and government voucher plans. Too many parents still believe that the government should educate their children at no cost to them.

Nevertheless, the homeschool movement as it exists today represents a triumph of parental independence and enterprise. Freedom lovers must do all in their power to support it and help it grow.

Index

A

Ach, M 37–38
Adam 126
Addams, Jane 8
AIDS 103–104, 158
Allport, Gordon 84
Alpha-Phonics vii, 33, 40
American
  Association of Colleges for
    Teacher Education
    (AACTE) 156
  Economic Association 5
  Fabian, The 7
  Historical Association 61, 70
  Humanist Association 74
  Journal of Education 117
  Political Science Association
    60
  Psychological Association 25
America's Secret Establishment 69
Angell, James R. 55
Anglicans 68
Animal Intelligence 26, 49
Aquarian Conspiracy, The 136
Association for Death Education
    and Counseling 145
Atheism 5, 43, 58, 95, 115
Atlantic Monthly, The 19, 144

B

Barnard, Henry 92
Beard, Charles 19
Becker, Tara 143–144

Beethoven 106
Behaviorism 49, 56
Behaviorism, -ists 30–32,
    56–57, 84, 90, 105–106,
    120
Belt, Carol 136
Bennett, William 53
Bernall, Cassie 139
Besant, Annie 3
Bible, The 23, 53, 67–68, 75,
    76, 82, 120, 124, 127,
    137, 139, 159–160, 166
Bibliotherapy 85
Blacker, David 117
Blavatsky, Helena 7
Bloom, Benjamin 84, 90,
    120–121, 129
Boodin, J. E. 59
Boston Globe 140
Boyette, Grant 140
Bragg, Raymond B. 93
Brennan, William J. 43
Brokaw, Tom 84
Buckley, William F., Jr. 70
Buschman, Harold 93
Bush, George, [Sr.] 70, 77
Bush, George W. 75, 77, 82,
    165
Butler, Nicholas Murray 92

C

Calvinism, -ists 23, 63–64,
    66–67, 71, 91
Calvin, John 22
Carneal, Michael 139
Carter, Jimmy 76

About the Author

Samuel L. Blumenfeld has spent the last 30 years writing about American education and seeking answers to such baffling questions as: Why is America experiencing a decline in literacy? Why are so many American children afflicted with learning disabilities? Why are the schools pushing sex ed, drug ed, and Ritalin, but are dead-set against intensive phonics and rote memorization of arithmetic facts?

His six previous books on education answer these and many more questions puzzling the public. His best-selling expose of the National Educational Association, *N.E.A. Trojan Horse in American Education*, has virtually become a classic in critical educational literature. Peter Brimelow, in *Fortune* magazine, called *Is Public Education Necessary?* brilliant revisionist history, and *How to Tutor and Alpha-Phonics* are being used by thousands of parents and homeschoolers to teach their children the 3R's in the traditional manner.

Born, and educated in New York City, Dr. Blumenfeld graduated from The City College of New York in 1950 and worked for ten years in the book publishing industry. His articles have appeared in many publications, and he has lectured and held seminars in all fifty states and Canada, England, Australia, and New Zealand. He has also tutored and taught in private schools and as a substitute in public schools. He is, no doubt, one of the world's leading authorities on the teaching of reading. In 1986 he was awarded an honorary Doctor of Laws degree by Bob Jones University.

The Ministry of Chalcedon

CHALCEDON (kal-see-don) is a Christian educational organization devoted exclusively to research, publishing, and cogent communication of a distinctively Christian scholarship to the world at large. It makes available a variety of services and programs, all geared to the needs of interested ministers, scholars, and laymen who understand the proposition that Jesus Christ speaks to the mind as well as the heart, and that His claims extend beyond the narrow confines of the various institutional churches. We exist in order to support the efforts of all orthodox denominations and churches. Chalcedon derives its name from the great ecclesiastical Council of Chalcedon (AD 451), which produced the crucial Christological definition: "Therefore, following the holy Fathers, we all with one accord teach men to acknowledge one and the same Son, our Lord Jesus Christ, at once complete in Godhead and complete in manhood, truly God and truly man...." This formula directly challenges every false claim of divinity by any human institution: state, church, cult, school, or human assembly. Christ alone is both God and man, the unique link between heaven and earth. All human power is therefore derivative: Christ alone can announce that, "All power is given unto me in heaven and in earth" (Matthew 28:18). Historically, the Chalcedonian creed is therefore the foundation of Western liberty, for it sets limits on all authoritarian human institutions by acknowledging the validity of the claims of the One who is the source of true human freedom (Galatians 5:1).

The Chalcedon Foundation publishes books under its own name and that of Ross House Books. It produces a magazine, Faith for All of Life, and a newsletter, Chalcedon Report, both bimonthly. All gifts to Chalcedon are tax deductible. For complimentary trial subscriptions, or information on other book titles, please contact:

Chalcedon
P.O. Box 158 • Vallecito, CA 95251 • USA • 209-736-4365
email: chalcedon@att.net • www.chalcedon.edu

Breinigsville, PA USA
27 August 2009
222990BV00003B/2/P